THE QUEST FOR MEANING

THE QUEST FOR MEANING

DARREN V KOCH

Copyright © 2025 by Darren V Koch
All rights reserved. No part of this book may be reproduced in any manner whatsoever without written permission except in the case of brief quotations embodied in critical articles and reviews.
First Printing, 2025

Cover photograph by Vincent Jewell

Contents

Acknowledgements	1
Author's Note	2
Introduction	3
To my Grandchildren	8
1 The Quest For Meaning	9
2 The Limits of Reason	22
3 The Leap of Faith	35
4 The Creek With Three Banks	42
5 Symbolic Language	58
6 Scripture and Tradition	71
7 Jesus Of Nazareth	81
8 Jesus: The Great Dilemma	102
9 Giving your Heart to Jesus	127
10 Who is Jesus?	145
11 Trinity: The Nature Of Reality	161
12 Love	177
13 Living in Love	189

14	Pain, Suffering and God	199
15	Prayer	223
16	Discernment	233
17	Death and Beyond	249
	Conclusion: The Signs of The Times	262

Select Bibliography   266

Acknowledgements

This book grew out of an entire life's journey. Beginning with my parents, Kingsley and Judy Koch, who set me on the first steps. Questions of meaning were not taboo for them, and they showed me, through their love that there was meaning in life.

My sister Valerie was my partner and companion on the journey for my most formative years. Together we struggled and questioned, seeking God and meaning. I will always be grateful for her love, and her wisdom.

I was fortunate to have many wonderful teachers and lecturers who challenged my youthful certainties and called me to live a meaningful life.

A special thanks goes to Joan Popjoy, who took a leap of faith and came to St. Bedes to speak to my year 12 Class in 1978. That decision changed my life, and I will be forever grateful.

My many friends, students and colleagues who journeyed with me as we fumbled our way towards wisdom together. I am grateful that you were part of my journey.

My former students, Natasha Dewhurst and Celeste Deliyiannis who first encouraged me to write this, and Vincent Jewell and Anna Demetriou who read the first drafts.

And finally my wonderful partner Jen Mansfield who painstakingly read each chapter and applied her devastating critiques. You elevated my assignment from a Pass to a Distinction, just like you elevate my life.

Author's Note

*In this book, I will use the word "God" often.
You may already have in your mind a fairly solid image
of what you think I mean when I talk about God.
But here's a very important fact that you need to understand
as you're reading this book;*

*The image of God that we have in our minds, is not God.
No matter what we imagine God to be,
What we have in our imagination is not God.
God is always something else.*

*For example, most people think of God as male.
When we use a pronoun for God we usually use "he" or "him".
But in his book, I use female pronouns for God.
You may find this jarring, and that's good.
When I'm talking about God in this book,
I'm not talking about your image of God or my image of God.
I'm talking about the ultimate source of all meaning.*

*God is not male. God is not Female.
God is both. And God is neither.*

Introduction

Dear Reader,

I taught Religious Education (R.E.) in Catholic schools for 25 years. In that time I refined my beliefs, read widely and by the end of my time had a pretty clear view about the content that I thought needed to be in any Religious Education Program at the dawn of the 21 century.

I feel a bit ashamed writing a book about the quest for meaning. I am no expert in these matters. I'm not an academic and the more I work on this book, the more I realise how much I lack in literacy and theology. But I firmly believe that the things I taught my students over those years are really important for a person to live a full and happy life.

I have been asked to write this book by many of my former students and they are my first audience. I've heard many of them say, "I wish I had a book with all the stuff we did in R.E."

Well... to a large extent, that is what this book is. An explanation of the most important things I taught in R.E in language that teenagers can understand. Several of my former students are now teaching in Catholic schools. I know that I would have liked a book like this to help me when I started my teaching career. So this book is for them.

Secondly, I offer this book to any young person struggling for meaning in their life. The quest for meaning is a lonely journey. The vast majority of people in my society refuse to take even one step.

I remember when I was in year 12, the main characters in all the books we studied seemed to wrestle with the problem of a meaningless life. Our teacher would talk about the need for meaning all the time.

"If you don't find it there," he'd say, gesturing towards the school chapel, "You need to find it in yourself."

I had no idea how the school chapel would provide meaning in my life. It was cool in the summer... and peaceful with silent wooden statues and a faint, comforting smell of incense. But meaning?

One day, I stayed behind after class and waited while he discussed essays, corrections and the questions of other students. Finally, when everyone had gone I asked, "What do you think the meaning of life is?"

He laughed shortly, a little bit uncomfortable.

I kept staring at him, waiting for his answer.

Then he got serious and said. "I think the meaning of life is to become the best we can be in every aspect."

I stared at him, waiting for him to continue.

He didn't.

I don't know if he could see the disappointment on my face. But there was certainly disappointment in my heart. That gave me no more clues than the cool, dim, chapel across the walkway. I nodded, thanked him for his answer and left the room.

But my yearning did not go away.

Later that year, my family went to my Uncle and Aunt's place for dinner. In addition to the adults, there was my older brother and sister, and my three older cousins. My cousins were the smartest people

I knew. They had gone to University. One was a teacher and another was doing his PhD.

When there was a break in the conversation, I asked, "What's the meaning of life?"

Silence descended. Everybody looked at me but I couldn't read the expressions on their faces. Were they blank? Were they shocked? Did they not think I was serious? Or did they just not know how to answer?

After a moment, someone started talking about something else and the dinner went on as if nothing had happened.

I stared at my plate wondering if I had made some sort of social faux pa.

Then, one of my cousins leaned across and looked deep into my eyes. "Don't ask questions like that," he said, softly. "You'll end up putting your head in an oven."

But my yearning did not go away.

Many of us crush down our yearning for meaning, not only in ourselves but in anyone around us. These are questions that we don't ask in polite company. Life is about making money, acquiring possessions, gaining status and experiencing pleasure. Don't ask for meaning.

Now, in my 60's, I have a slightly better understanding than I did when I was a bemused teenager. My generation and the generations above and below me have been smothered in a mire of consumption. We have seemingly unlimited energy, ceaseless entertainment, access to vast amounts of goods, foods and delicacies from every corner of the world. We are drowning in a foetid swamp of mindless consumption.

Very few of us raise a hand above the water to call for help, and often those that do, receive either no response or worse, they get entrapped by some toxic wold-view that leaves them in a worse place than they were before. This book is written for all those who raise their hand and cry out for meaning.

I don't expect many of this generation to raise their hand. We have too many possessions, too much power, too many distractions. The shiny lights, the bells and whistles of our age keep our hands firmly on the mouse and keyboard. Not many hands are free to reach up.

But this era of consumption is coming to an end. We found a mighty store of fossil energy and we have been burning it furiously for nearly 200 years. We've been dancing naked around the fire in ecstatic abandon, but the fire is going out. Soon we will be left cold and exposed to the brutal realities of life. Then, maybe we will ask the questions we have been avoiding. Why are we here? Where did we come from? Where are we going? What is the meaning of all this?

This leads to the third audience of this book. Those who will reach adolescence in the 2030's and 2040's. This book is written with an eye firmly set on the future. The generation that will see the fire dying are toddlers now. Being raised as if the fire will go on forever, being told that they will be able to dance, just like their parents and grand parents did. But they will find that the easy promises of consumption, greed and cheap energy were lies, and their grief will be terrible.

I can't express in words how sad this makes me. This morning, as I was in the shower and planning to write this section, I put my face in my hands and sobbed with grief and shame. My generation has failed you. I am so very sorry.

You will need to make the journey, to undertake the quest for meaning. In my day there are many misleading voices clambering for attention, offering dead end pathways. Religious groups with simplistic but toxic answers. Materialists who make despair a virtue. Hedonists who would cover up their yearning with brittle laughter. I don't expect these voices to go away in the next 20 years, so this book is designed to help you find your way through them. Consider it a faint attempt to atone for the failures of my generation.

Finally, this third audience contains my grandchildren and this the literary device that I am using to convey my message. The quest for meaning is not just an intellectual exercise. It occurs first and foremost within the context of a relationship. As I take you on this journey, dear reader, I want you to feel like you are part of a relationship. I want you to feel like you are part of my family. Because you are. Because we belong to each other. Even if you've never met me, or never spoken a single word to me, we are family. We are one people, on one planet, in one Cosmos. We are one.

I'll explain more about why and how that is later on, but for now, just suspend disbelief. Imagine I am your grandfather. Imagine I love you. Imagine, I've written this book for you because I thought that maybe one day you will need it. And when you do, it will be here waiting for you.

This love letter from a grandfather you never met.

To my Grandchildren

Darling Kingsley, Turi, Daisy, Felix, Raf, Hugo and Ezren,
A few years before Turi and Daisy were born, your mum/ Aunt Jess and I were talking about the environment and how bad things were looking. Your mum said, "With the world in such a bad way, I wonder if it's the right thing to do to have children. What world are we bringing them into?" This idea has been quite common in recent years. Many of your parents' generation have decided not to have children for just that reason.

I will never forget her face at that moment. So open and vulnerable, filled with love for you even before you were conceived. At that moment, I felt something stir deep within my soul. I knew that even though there were too many of us and the future looked bleak, there were bigger forces at play. A deeper fire burned beneath the surface. You were meant to be born. You are not an irresponsible consumer item that your parents wanted. And you are not just the result of an irresistible biological urge to reproduce. You are the product of a Great Love. You have been called into existence for a reason. Your life matters.

As I sit here in my little farm in Gippsland watching our civilisation unravel and the great tide of secular ignorance sweep across our land, I am convinced that the things I taught my students will become even more important in the next few decades and I believe in my deepest heart that you will need this before the end.

Love
Grandpa

1

The Quest For Meaning

Does Life Have Meaning?

"Death makes everything meaningless."

I used to begin my year 8 Religious Education class by writing that quote on the board. The statement is a simplified paraphrase of a french Philosopher, Albert Camus. I would then invite the kids to disagree. They would try to justify the meaning of their lives as I took Camus' position. Sometimes the discussion would start off slowly and I'd have to talk a bit to get them started. I'd talk about humanity's instinctive denial of death. I would say something like this:

> *If you go to any adult and say to them, "I'm going to die one day", you can bet that their response will include two words: 'yes' and 'but'.*

'Yes, but you don't have to worry about that now.' Or 'Yes, but *it's the life you live that matters.' 'Yes, but...' 'Yes but...' How about 'Yes and...!' Surely the wisest response should begin with 'Yes and...'*

Camus says, Death makes everything meaningless, so according to Camus, your life is meaningless. Everything you do is pointless. Why do we bother? One day every one of us will be dead. And once we're dead, what will it matter what we did in our year 8 Religion Class?

That would usually start the kids off. They would often begin with the argument that they would do things in their life that mattered.

"Like what?" I'd ask.

"I could become a doctor and save people's lives."

"Doctors don't save people's lives," I'd say. "What do you think happens to all the people whose lives are saved by doctors? They die! And their death makes their life just as meaningless as the doctor's."

"But we could make the world a better place while we are alive. Feed the hungry or care for Earth."

I'd tap on the board and continue: Camus is not saying that your death makes everything meaningless. He's saying Death itself makes everything meaningless. The whole world is doomed to die. In about 800 million years the Sun will expand, swallowing Mercury and baking Venus to a crisp. The heat will burn off Earth's atmosphere and Earth will become a scalded dead world. There will be no sign of life here. No schools, no hospitals, no butterflies. A vast desolate furnace. Once that happens, what difference does it make if you protected a species or planted a tree?

At this point, there would almost always be someone who launches into the Star Trek fantasy, i.e., "We might have developed interstellar space flight by then and we'd be living on other planets."

"Maybe," I'd say. "But all those planets are tied to stars, just like ours. And they too will grow old, and die. Eventually all the stars in the all the galaxies will go out and the universe will become cold, dark and lifeless. When the universe is nothing more than a collection of countless black holes drifting silently through space, what will it matter what a bunch of primates did on earth?

It's the law of entropy. Every fire goes out, every cup of coffee goes cold, every living thing dies and decomposes into compost. Every ordered system breaks down to its simplest and least energetic form. Death is entropy and it's an iron clad scientific law in our universe. Death has the last word. Always has and always will. That's why Camus says that life is meaningless. Camus says that the biggest question we must ask ourselves is whether or not to commit suicide.

You can imagine how this went down with my 13-year-old audience at the start of their school year.. Usually there would be a stunned silence. Often someone would break the tension with a joke, "I might throw myself off a bridge."

I would let the laughter and jokes run because laughter is an important element when we are staring into the abyss. In fact, if the kids didn't break the tension, I would. I'd continue to run the argument but I'd run it more like a stand up comedy routine than a lecture. Soon we'd all be discussing the futility of life and laughing about it. I remember in one class a boy said, "I'm going to use this argument when Mum tells me to do the dishes. What does it matter if the dishes are washed? WE'RE ALL GONNA DIE!" It would often become a common line: Kochie's R.E. class makes you want to commit suicide.

Once the laughter had run its course, I'd become serious.

Camus didn't believe in God. He thought life is meaningless because Death has the last word. Christians don't believe that death has the last word. We believe that God has the last word. But whether you're a believer or an unbeliever, we all rebel against the idea that we live in a meaningless world. Nobody wants a meaningless life. We all want our lives to matter. Some people even commit suicide when they believe their life is meaningless. A meaningless life is terrifying.

It's amazing that in the ten years I taught that lesson, not once did a student run the hedonistic argument, i.e., "Yeah, we're all going to die, so we might as well have fun and enjoy it while we live". It was as if they instinctively knew the horror of that point of view. When confronted with the philosophical implications of death, every class, every student tried to justify their existence by doing good for others.

Personally, I find this deeply comforting. Maybe it was because I taught in a Catholic school and even though my students weren't very religious, they all had imbibed some of the Christian ethos. Maybe things are different now, maybe the despair has soaked into our children's bones. Maybe. But I like to think that deep in the human heart, we know that Goodness is intricately bound up with the question of meaning.

Everywhere we go in our society the hedonistic argument is thrown at us. We tell ourselves again and again, that life is about pleasure. Every advertisement, every action movie, every corporate management plan, has the terrible subtext – Life is meaningless, but have fun. Consume and seek pleasure. We poison our children with it, and then we wonder why we are all so sad.

Walk through any shopping centre and look into the eyes of the people shopping. They are surrounded by wealth and resources unimaginable to our ancestors, but in the midst of all that excess, there is a devastating emptiness in our souls. We live meaningless lives and our hearts are empty because of it.

We need meaning in our lives. Despite our limited, finite nature, humans yearn for the infinite. It is this yearning for ultimate meaning that drives the religious quest.

The Yearning For Meaning

At this point, I'd like to take a moment to consider what may have been going on in your heart that has led you to start reading this book.

You've picked up a book on the meaning of life and have read the introduction and into the first chapter. You are definitely seeking meaning in your life. Something deep in your soul is yearning for it. Perhaps there was a time when you felt no need for meaning, or maybe you once thought your life had meaning and now it no longer does. Maybe the question of meaning in life has been nagging at you for a long time. Maybe this is the first time you've been confronted with the question, or maybe you've picked up this book because the question has only recently begun to haunt you. Whatever your past, you have now begun a quest for meaning that is driven by a deep yearning.

What can we say about this yearning? It seems to me that this yearning can only be interpreted in two ways. Firstly, it may be some form of psychological dysfunction. A kind of mild mental illness, where you crave something that doesn't exist. From this perspective, your desire for meaning is merely a passing phase. Those people who never struggle with the question are more stable than you. They have moved beyond childish desires and accepted the world as it is. Someday, you too will get over this desire and realise that life just is. There is no meaning to it and you shouldn't feel the need for meaning.

The second interpretation is the yearning for meaning, is deeply entrenched in the human condition. All rational, self-conscious beings must ask questions about meaning and purpose. The desire for meaning is inherent in human nature and whilst it can be repressed, the repression is profoundly unhealthy. According to this point of view, those who argue for the first position (i.e., our yearning for meaning is a psychological dysfunction), are crushing down a crucial part of what makes them human. Their lives are poorer because they are denying their innermost nature. They are like a person who permanently wears a blindfold. Eventually, their capacity to see gets lost and light itself becomes painful.

Of course, you can probably guess that I strongly advocate the second position. Humans are meaning making creatures. This is hard wired into our minds. How can we say that we are allowed us to ask "why" about small things like 'Why does a plant die if doesn't get water?' but not about bigger things like, 'Why are there plants at all?'

But be aware, even if the yearning for meaning is inherent to the human condition, it doesn't mean that life and the universe has some objective meaning. This deep yearning for meaning could be nothing more than a quirk of evolution brought about by our capacity to reason. We could all still be living meaningless lives in a meaningless universe. We are on a quest and we don't know if the thing we're searching for exists or not.

But I do not believe that we live meaningless lives in a meaningless universe. I believe that the yearning in your heart is there because the whole universe pulsates with meaning. You only have to open your eyes to see the patterns, the connections, the great purpose. It all makes sense, it just doesn't all make sense to me or you.

Because you are part of this world, the depth of your soul is responding to the depth of the whole universe. The quest for meaning is not a question which has a simple answer. It's more like embarking on a journey across a vast landscape, like crossing a continent where the more you discover, the more you realise you don't know.

Trust the yearning in your heart, my darlings. Don't fear it. Don't deny it. It's part of you. It's good. It's healthy. It will lead you to wisdom.

Meaning and Purpose

As we begin our quest for meaning, it's probably important to say a few words about the nature of meaning and how it is similar to, but different from, purpose.

Any sentient being can have a purpose. My purpose at the moment is to write this book for you. Somewhere in the paddock outside my house, a fox may have a purpose to catch and eat my neighbour's chickens. You may wish to commit your life to collecting all the marbles in the world and store them in your back shed. I may think that is not a very good thing to dedicate your life to, but if it's your purpose and you're happy with it, who am I to criticise?

But when we come to ask for meaning, we are then asking about something deeper, more profound than just purpose. Any sentient being can give itself purpose, but nothing can give itself meaning. For a being to have meaning, there must be some higher order of reality in which it resides.

Imagine, I come up to you and say, "*Slartibartfast.*" Does that word mean anything?

There are two aspects to this. Firstly, the only way that a word can mean something is if it is part of a larger system of words we call "a language." A language is a higher order of being than simply a single word. Secondly for *Slartibartfast* to have any meaning, this language must be known by more than one person. The word must be meaningful to someone. Without that someone, the word has no meaning.

So, when we talk about our lives having meaning, we are asking firstly if there is a higher order of reality where our life fits, and secondly, if there is any Other that understands the meaning of our lives. This is different from purpose. Some people talk of meaning as "a higher purpose." That phrase hints at the concept of ultimate meaning but it doesn't capture it fully.

Now if you've been to a Catholic school or been raised in a theistic environment, you may be assuming that I'm taking here about God, but I'm not. There are many people whose life fits into a larger or higher order of being without it being God. A person can feel that their life is given meaning by their family. Another could find in their nation the higher order that gives their life meaning. A third person may feel that they belong within the entire natural world and this is what gives their life meaning.

The trouble with all these bases of meaning is that Albert Camus' argument shoots them down. For our lives to have ultimate meaning, there must be something that is not going to be swept away by time into the nothingness of death. According to Camus, if there is nothing that can transcend death, then everything is truly meaningless. Only a frame of meaning that is not subject to death can refute Camus.

Meaning and God

Imagine we are walking through the bush and we come upon a large rock. On the face of the rock the following is carved:

Η αγάπη είναι η πηγή και το πεπρωμένο μας

What does it mean? Does it mean anything? It looks like writing; there seems to be words and spaces, like writing, but is there a meaning or a concept behind it? We can stare at the carving all day and not get any closer to working out its meaning. To fully understand what this means, we have to know the context. Who or what carved it? Why did they carve it? Is it a language? If so, which one? Without this knowledge of context, this carving is just a collection of abstract symbols with no discernible meaning.

Life is like that. We are faced with a universe that seems to have patterns and structure deeply embedded within it, but we have no idea what it all means, or if it means anything at all. This is because we can't go outside of our universe to see the context. We don't know who or what caused the universe. We don't know why it was caused or why it exists. We don't know if there is any purpose to it.

If we consider ourselves as part of the universe, this same line of questioning can be applied to us. Why are we here? What do we mean? What is our purpose? Do we matter at all? There seems to be no way to answer these questions by studying ourselves or the universe. We only know that we crave meaning and purpose in our lives. This is the tragedy of the human condition. We are thinking beings who yearn for meaning. We are thrown into a universe that seems to hint at order, pattern and intelligibility. And yet, we can't work out if the universe, or our life, means anything at all.

C.S. Lewis was a Christian thinker from the middle of last century. You may know him as the author of the Narnia book series, but he was also a highly respected academic and theologian. Lewis argues that our yearning for meaning is a sign that meaning exists. We are products of this universe, so it makes sense that we would only yearn for things that exist within the universe. For example, we have hunger because there is food. There is thirst because there is water. There is sexual desire because there is sex. There is loneliness because there is companionship. So, if we yearn for meaning, there must be meaning.

But Albert Camus says death makes everything meaningless. He's right, but only to some extent. At the heart of Camus' argument is the assumption that death itself is meaningless. But death is an intrinsic part of life, part of the finite universe. So, if there is meaning in the universe, then death too must mean something. But what?

Like with the carvings on the rock, if we are to find meaning in the universe, we must go beyond the universe. We must find context. In short, our yearning for meaning and purpose in our lives takes us directly to a yearning for a creator God, a divine Author that provides that context.

It's important to realise at this point, that I'm not making any claims about God. I am simply defining God as *"the source of meaning for all that is."* God is the language and the author that gives the sentence meaning.

Does this help us? Instead of chasing our tails, searching for a meaning we can't grasp, we are now chasing our tails searching for a God who may not exist.

People have argued about the existence of God for centuries. In the last century or so, this debate intensified. Nowadays, the internet is full of strident voices insisting that their particular world view is absolutely correct and that opposing views are completely wrong. One thing all these voices have in common, is a bizarre certainty about things humans simply can't understand.

The universe is really, really big. Life is incredibly complex. Do we seriously believe that our simple primate minds can grasp the fundamental nature of reality? We seem to behave as if the ground and horizon of all being can be explained using our limited language. What arrogance! What absolute hubris! Be very careful about anyone who claims to have certainty in these matters. They are either lying, or deluded. The path of wisdom leads us through the jungle of uncertainty. It's scary and humans don't like it. But there is no other way to go.

2

The Limits of Reason

Science and Religion

Our culture has great confidence in reason. The sharpest focus of human reason is expressed through science. You will often hear people say, "I don't believe in religion. I believe in science," as if belief in one excludes belief in the other. This is a very common attitude and even some highly intelligent, educated people hold this view. But this attitude misunderstands both the nature of religion and the nature of science.

Imagine a little girl comes home from kindergarten and finds a chocolate cake on the kitchen bench. The cake has four candles on it and is laced with cream and icing.

"Why is this here?" She asks.

Her older brother explains, "When you take flour and mix it with water and an egg, it forms a batter. And if you heat that batter at 180 degrees Celsius for about 40 minutes, it turns into a cake."

Her older sister laughs and cuffs the brother on the back of his head. "Mum made it for you because it's your birthday and we are celebrating because we all love you."

Both the brother and the sister told the truth, and both of them tried to answer the little girl's question. But the brother answered the 'how' not the 'why'. The brother took the scientific path while the sister took the religious one.

Science and religion are two different ways of looking at the world. It's not that one is right and the other is wrong. It's just that they wrestle with different questions and use different methods to answer them. The science versus religion debate occurs when people try to use religion to answer scientific questions and science to answer religious ones. Science can't answer religious questions and religion can't answer scientific ones.

In the example above, there is no way that science could answer that little girl's question. We could break up the cake, analyse the chemical compounds or use microbiological testing to estimate its freshness. We would still find no evidence to tell us that it's the little girl's birthday or if her mother loved her. Scientific analysis on the cake can't answer that question.

With our limited language, we often ask why something is the way it is, when in fact we want to know how. For example; many children ask the question "why is the sky blue?" On the face of it, we assume that it is a scientific question, i.e., What causes the sky to appear blue?

But what if the question was asked in an artist's studio? If I was watching a painter creating a landscape and I asked, "why is the sky blue?", then it would be a very different question. I could be asking about the meaning and purpose of the artist's work. The artist might say, "I chose to make it blue to contrast with the red coat of the man in the foreground," or they may say, "no reason... I just have a lot of spare blue paint."

The last two and a half centuries have been a time of breathtaking scientific development. Questions that previously seemed mysterious and beyond our understanding have now been explored and plausible theories have been proposed. The power of this scientific revolution has led many people to believe there is no question that cannot be answered by science and reason. But despite our intellectual power, human reason has limits.

The Limits of Reason

In the 1640's René Descartes began publishing his work on Mathematics and Philosophy, making a profound impact on Western Society. Not many people know or care much about his ideas nowadays, but the most important part of his philosophy was his method.

Descartes argued that all faith and tradition is dubious. He adopted a position of universal doubt and argued the only way we could know something with certainty was through our reason. Descartes' philosophical method can be summarised as, *'truth can only be accessed using reason'*. This was the beginning of what has been called the Enlightenment, when European thinkers began to apply only reason in their quest for truth.

This reliance on reason and the quest for certainty lead to the modern philosophical belief of *Rationalism*. Rationalism often goes a step further than Descartes. Instead of assuming that 'Truth can only be accessed using reason', rationalists sometimes act as if *Reason can access all truth*. In other words, an extreme Rationalist would say, *'Only that which can be rationally proven is true'*.

Let's pause for a moment and look at this carefully.
There are three different positions here:
A. Something that can be rationally proven must be true.
B. Truth can only be accessed by reason.
C. Only that which can be rationally proven is true.

I don't think there is anyone who seriously doubts position A. Descartes held position B but many philosophers disagree with him. Position C is representative of an extreme form of rationalism which is commonly referred to as *Scientism*.

It is this belief that leads many very intelligent and well-educated people to argue that if there is no scientific proof for something, it therefore must not exist. Even some scientists hold this belief. The argument is very powerful and many people of my generation hold to it quite fiercely, but there is a big problem with their position that completely undermines their argument. Let me show you what it is.

The statement, *'Only that which can be proved by science or reason is true'* cannot be proven either scientifically or rationally. Therefore, by its own logic it is false. (Go back and read those two previous sentences again. They're important.) The statement is a belief. It has no basis in reason or science. It's just pure faith, but it's not a very good faith because the statement can't be true.

Let's analyse the argument this way:

A. Only that which can be proved by science or reason is true.

B. Statement A cannot be proved by science or reason.

C. Therefore if Statement A is true, it must be false.

It's not a good idea to build a philosophical worldview on the basis of a statement which cannot be true according to its own logic. There is nothing wrong with statements of faith. Humans use them all the time and we simply couldn't function without them. But for a statement of faith to be worthwhile, there must be at least a possibility that it is true. A statement of faith that is demonstrably false cannot provide any basis for a meaningful life.

Scientism or rationalism is very attractive because it offers us certainty and human beings love certainty. Unfortunately for us, uncertainty is a fundamental part of the human condition. We don't know where we came from, we don't know where we are going and we don't know if anything we do matters. We are staring at scrawls carved into the rock face and we don't know if it means anything.

In 1781, Immanuel Kant wrote his philosophical masterpiece, <u>The Critique of Pure Reason</u>. Put simply, Kant argued that human reason has definite limits. There are things which reason can show us and there are things that reason cannot show us. It is interesting that even though Kant would not consider himself a Christian, in this respect Kant led secular philosophy back to the Judaeo-Christian position which is that we need both Faith and Reason to access truth.

In mainstream Christian theology, faith and reason are the two wings of a bird. The bird can't fly with only one. In the same way, in our quest for meaning, we will need both faith and reason.

The First Cause Argument

Humans are finite beings who long for the infinite. We want our lives to have meaning but we don't know if they do. For our lives to have meaning, there must be something that gives them meaning. A context, a creator to which we owe our existence. Like the scrawls on the rock wall, the scrawls can't give themselves meaning. Meaning can only be given by the one who created them.

Remember: At this stage we are defining God only as "the source of meaning for all that is". We are not making any other claims about the nature of God.

So, is there an author and a language for the universe? Is there a creator God? The short answer is that we don't know, but people insist on arguing about it as if one person's reason can convince another. I'm not going to go into all the 'ins and outs' of that dead end debate, but I want to make a very important point here, both the theist and the atheist positions are reasonable. Theists aren't irrational or ignorant, and atheists aren't blind to reality. If we are going to seriously address the question of meaning, we need to accept that there is no provable answer to the question. There is no room for certainty on this quest.

To illustrate this, I will now go on to explore the pros and cons of the most useful popular argument for the existence of God, The First Cause Argument.

This is an old argument (most of the arguments for and against God are old). Early forms can be found in the Old Testament and the writings of Ancient Greek philosophers. But the argument has been most clearly laid out by the great

Catholic theologian, Thomas Aquinas in the 13th century. In a simple form it runs like this:

> Everything in the Universe has a beginning.
> Everything that has a beginning has a cause.
> To avoid an infinite regress, there must be a first cause that was not caused by any other being.
> And this we understand to be God.

Let's unpack this a bit slower. Everything that we know of in the universe, has come into existence. Think about all the animals, the plants, the rocks, the stars, the galaxies. There was a time when all these things did not exist. They had a beginning. And each of these things were caused by other forces or beings.

On my desk beside me is a hot cup of tea. Twenty minutes ago, that cup of tea didn't exist in its current form. There was water in the water tank, a kettle attached to a power source in my kitchen, and a tea bag in my pantry. I put these things together and caused a cup of tea to come into existence. So we can say that the cup of tea was 'caused' by the water, the kettle, the power, the tea bag and me. All these factors combined to cause the cup of tea.

For simplicity's sake, let's just concentrate on the water in the tank as a cause of the cup of tea. There was a time when the water wasn't in the tank. Heat from the sun caused it to be evaporated from the surface of the earth and gathered into clouds. Then the water fell as rain onto my roof, and was collected in my water tank.

But where did the water come from? There was a time, when those water molecules in my cup of tea didn't exist. According to contemporary scientific cosmology, the atoms of Hydrogen and Oxygen that combined to make up the water in my cup of tea were formed within an ancient star. Nuclear fusion in the heart of these early stars created all the elements that exist today.

But there was a time when that primitive star did not exist. It too was caused. Gravitational forces caused hydrogen and helium to cluster into huge clouds. Eventually these gravitational forces caused the nuclear fusion and it ignited.

But there was a time when the Hydrogen did not exist. The Hydrogen was caused when sub-atomic particles, protons and electrons, joined together to form the first atoms. Scientists say that these sub atomic particles were all caused in the big bang. A single instant when all the known universe was compressed into a single, unimaginably hot point.

In a simplistic form, the First Cause argument, can be expressed as 'what caused the big bang?'

According to American ethnobotanist, Terence McKenna: "Modern science is based on the principle: 'Give us one free miracle and we'll explain the rest.' The one free miracle is the appearance of all the mass and energy in the universe and all the laws that govern it in a single instant from nothing." This is a form of the first cause argument, but it's embedded in our contemporary scientific paradigm.

We need to be very careful here. Contemporary cosmology is pretty robust and it is the best scientific understanding that we have at the moment. But there is no guarantee that these theories are 100% correct. The current theory for the origin of the universe is the best explanation scientists have, at the moment. In 20 years, this theory could well be replaced by a new one. That's how science works. Always testing and refining. Always adapting as new evidence comes to light. Never static. Never certain.

Whether the 'big bang' is an accurate description of how the universe formed or not, the philosophical problem remains. *How can something come from nothing?* Thomas Aquinas says that the universe didn't pop into existence from nothing. He says it comes from God.

Arguments Against The First Cause

The first cause argument is very common. When I was a kid in primary school, my best friend was an atheist. We used to argue about the existence of God and I used a simple version of the first cause argument. My friend replied with one of the most common objections to it... "*Who made God?*"

If everything has a cause and the first cause was God, then what caused God? This argument was not thought up by an 11-year-old in 1971. It's been made often throughout history by many intelligent people, including the famous philosopher Bertrand Russell. Russell argued that if we assert everything has a cause, but then allow God to be exempted from needing a cause, we could just as easily say that the universe itself was the thing without a cause. This is a very good rebuttal but it's not conclusive.

The First Cause argument doesn't assert that everything has a cause. It states that everything that has a beginning, has a cause. The idea that something can just pop into existence without a cause goes against the most fundamental principles of science and experience. This is what's called a properly basic belief.

But it only takes a small tweak to make Russell's argument sound. If the first cause argument states that everything in the universe has a beginning, maybe the universe itself has no beginning. It is possible to imagine an eternal universe without a beginning.

The idea that the universe popped into existence, uncaused, flies in the face of common sense and that is why some of our brightest scientific minds are trying to explain Terence

McKenna's free miracle. One day the bright minds may succeed. But the problem won't go away. Whatever we find that caused the big bang, a philosopher can ask, what caused it?

The most popular theory going around to explain the one free miracle is the idea of the *multiverse*. The idea of the multiverse is not new. Like so much of philosophy, it goes back to the ancient Greeks. In particular, it can be attributed to a philosopher named *Anaximander* in the 6th century BC.

The contemporary multiverse idea is that we live in only one of an infinite number of universes, each with their own space, time, matter, energy and information. Each of these universes has a beginning.

This is all too complex for me, but the best metaphor I can find for the multiverse theory is that the infinite universes 'float' like bubbles in a glass of lemonade. The 'lemonade' is some fundamental fabric of space-time that we don't understand. But it is uncaused and has no beginning. Out of this primal lemonade, pops 'bubbles' of universes.

The problem with the idea of the multiverse is that we cannot measure or test the hypothesis scientifically. As it cannot be falsified or verified, it's not scientific. It's a philosophical concept and we cannot prove its existence or non-existence. Sound familiar?

There's a whole area of thought and research on the idea of a multiverse but for our purposes, we can propose either an uncaused first cause that creates everything that has a beginning, or a primal 'lemonade' which gives birth to multiple universes. Both of these are beyond our reason and beyond science. Both positions are reasonable and we have no way of knowing which best describes reality.

I should point out, here that the 'eternal, uncaused lemonade' of the multiverse and the uncaused, first cause of theology could well be one and the same reality. But one world view implies the universe has meaning and the other does not. We are still standing in front of the rock wall, not knowing if the carvings were caused by a being with a mind and a message, or if it's the product of natural weathering with no meaning or purpose at all.

3

The Leap of Faith

A Logical Dead End.

Reason can only take us so far in our quest for meaning. We have reasoned our way to something which feels like a dead end. It's like we've been following the path of Reason through bushland and come to a creek shaped like an upside down Y. The path stops but we can still jump across the creek to either the left or the right side. Now we are faced with three alternatives.

i) We can sit down where we are and declare that we don't know.

ii) We can take a leap of faith and say, "There is no God and no meaning in life".

Or,

iii) We can take a different leap of faith and say, "There is God and there is meaning in life".

The first option gets us nowhere. We are just sitting on the bank of a creek unable to move. In actual fact, there is nothing wrong with staying here as long as you like. You don't have to take a leap if you don't want to, but eventually life will insist that you choose. You may be faced with a decision that relies on you having a philosophical position, or the yearning in your heart for some sort of meaning and purpose in your life may become too strong to resist. Then you will have to take a leap.

Once you take the leap in one direction or the other, there is nothing to stop you from turning around and going back. An educated person's worldview is constantly growing and changing as they go through their life. When I was a teenager, I had a very different worldview to the one I had when I was teaching. And the worldview I have now in my older years is different again. In your life, there is nothing to stop you from changing your mind.

Some of my students found these ideas a bit uncomfortable. They had been taught that God insists on us believing in Her and if we don't, She will punish us. Before we go on, we need to address this issue because it's crucial for our quest that we understand the difference between faith and opinion.

Faith and opinion

An opinion is a statement that we think is true based on our reason. But there are very few things that we actually know. Often when we say we know something, we are just confident in our opinion. But sometimes this confidence is misplaced. There are three broad categories of misplaced confidence and they are all related to the limits of reason.

Firstly, we have already established that there are some things that reason cannot know with certainty. When it comes to some questions, there are intrinsic limits to reason. Reason cannot tell us if life has meaning and reason cannot prove the existence of God. But even in our daily lives, reason has limits. When we fall in love and somebody tells us that they will love us forever, reason cannot tell us whether this promise will be kept. Even the person making the promise cannot be sure that they will follow through.

Secondly, we may think we know something but we're really only accepting the conventional wisdom of the day. When I was a kid, we were told that dinosaurs were cold blooded. I thought I knew that dinosaurs were cold blooded. When I was an adult, the scientific consensus changed and we were told that dinosaurs were warm blooded. As an adult, I thought I knew that dinosaurs were warm blooded. The fact is, I never knew whether dinosaurs were cold blooded or warm blooded. I've always just accepted the current scientific consensus. I was sharing everybody else's opinion.

Finally, there are some times when a person can think very hard about a question that reason should be able to answer, but they make an error of logic and they get their answer wrong.

When I did maths tests in high school, every question had a correct answer, and I did my best to work out that answer. But I never got 100% on any maths test. I always made a few mistakes. And the thing about making errors in reason, is that you don't know that you're making them. You do your best, and then you write down the answer. But you can't be sure that your answer is right. It's just your opinion.

Most people find uncertainty uncomfortable but some people react very badly to errors, mistakes and opinions they consider to be false. Some teachers punish their students when they get a question wrong. Some parents get angry at their children when they a mistake. Some people mock and look down on people who do not share their opinions. And some religious people project this unhealthy attitude onto God.

Faith: To Give your Heart to Something

Now, if you've had some experience of Christian teaching, you may be aware that Jesus often said that we must believe to be saved. We must have faith to be redeemed. And you'd be right. But what did Jesus and the fathers of the Church mean when they talked about belief?

Well, let's get this straight, when Jesus talked about faith or belief, he wasn't talking about opinion. Jesus never said you must have a certain opinion to be saved, even though many Christians assume that this is exactly what he meant. In fact, this is exactly what he did *not* mean.

Many Christians lump belief and opinion together. But Christian doctrine sees these things as being very different.

According to mainstream Christian Theology, to believe is to give your heart to something. Giving your heart to something is a bit like falling in love. It's not like doing a maths problem. It's a choice and an act of will but it also includes trust and hope. To believe in something is to act as if this thing were true even though you don't know if is.

When Jesus talked about faith, he wasn't interested in people's opinion. He wanted them to give their hearts. God is not interested in what our meagre intellect thinks about various religious controversies. She is passionately concerned about what we give our hearts to.

Let's think about it logically. God creates a universe such that no matter how hard we try or how honestly we pursue Her, we cannot work out whether She exists or not. Then She declares that we must jettison our reason and just believe She exists or else She will punish us. God sounds like a bit of a bloody monster, doesn't She?

What if a person in their deepest heart simply doesn't believe the Christian story? Does God insist that they lie to themselves and their community? That they pretend to believe? Not a very moral course of action is it.

Whatever your path in life, my darlings, it's very important that you are true to yourself. Believe what you believe, and live according to your beliefs. If God exists, and She wants you to believe something else, She can sort you out.

At this stage of my life, I actually suspect that God doesn't give a bugger what we think about life, the universe and everything. God is like a father watching his daughter playing with a stick in a sandpit. The dad doesn't care if she pretends the stick is a bulldozer, a cow or a person. So long as she don't poke the stick into her brother's eye, he's happy. Of course, if his daughter declared that stick to be a snake and traumatised herself or her brother, then I think the dad would be displeased. In our world there are plenty of imaginary snakes in our metaphorical sandpit. I'm writing this book to help you to avoid them.

I will return to this dichotomy between belief and opinion again later in this book, but for now, let's get back to the bank of the creek and decide which way to jump. We can jump in one of two directions. Either there is no God and no meaning, or else God exists and there is meaning.

We now find ourselves trapped between competing fears and yearnings. On the one hand, we yearn for meaning and are terrified of being cast adrift in a meaningless universe. But on the other hand, the only way for the universe to have meaning, is if there is a creator God who has imposed meaning on the universe. If there is a God who has imposed meaning on the universe, then we owe that creator allegiance.

Which do you fear more? Meaninglessness or having a Supreme Authority in the Universe? Which do you yearn for more? Meaning in your life or freedom to chart your own course? Can we have both?

4

The Creek With Three Banks

The Atheist Bank

Let's jump across the creek to where there is no God and life has no meaning. Don't be afraid, we can jump back again later. On this side of the bank, we have a problem. We are in a meaningless universe but deep in our hearts we still yearn for meaning. Can we survive in a world without meaning? Can we live a full life believing that death makes everything meaningless?

Albert Camus wrestled with this idea in his essay <u>The Myth of Sisyphus</u>. In Greek legend, Sisyphus was condemned by the gods to roll a large boulder up a steep hill. Whenever he pushed the boulder to the top of the hill, it was snatched from his grasp and it rolled back down into the valley. Sisyphus had to return to the bottom and roll the boulder up all over again. Camus argues that this is the human condition. Everything we do, eventually fails. All our loves, dreams, hopes and desires are eventually swallowed up in Death.

Camus argues that only by acknowledging the futility of his situation, can Sisyphus conquer it. He reaches a state of contented acceptance. He finds joy in the meaningless act of rolling the stone. Camus said,

"The struggle itself to the heights is enough to fill a man's heart. One must imagine Sisyphus happy."

When I used to tell my students this, I'd usually find myself staring into a classroom full of blank looks. I find Camus quite inspiring but for most of us, it's not a very satisfying way to live our lives. I'm sure there are men and women of great strength of character who can find joy in an utterly meaningless universe, while accepting their yearning for meaning. But I'm not one of them. It requires more strength of character than I possess.

In my experience, most people who have taken the leap across the creek into a meaningless world, deny their yearning for meaning. As a result, their lives become stunted and they are unable to cope when life throws up crises and catastrophe. And life does. You can take that to the bank. If you deny your yearning for meaning, it will not go away. It will haunt you.

There is, however, another alternative. American Academic, Joseph Campbell wrote, *"Life is without meaning. The meaning of life is whatever you ascribe it to be"*.

This alternative has become very popular in recent years. You'll find this worldview all over the place. Turn over any rock and you'll find someone declaring that we have to find our own meaning. The strength of this position is that it doesn't deny our yearning for meaning but it's weakness is that we know in our deepest heart, that any meaning we ascribe is not real. If life has no meaning, then any meaning we ascribe cannot true. We're just making it up.

So, what does it take to live a meaningful life on the atheist side of the creek? There seems to be a few things that any system of meaning needs.

Firstly, it must at least have the possibility of truth. There's no point creating a system of meaning not compatible with reality. Reality doesn't change just because we refuse to believe in it. Therefore, the system of meaning we adopt must be internally consistent, reasonable and compatible with reality as we experience it.

Secondly, the system of meaning must address the deep need in our hearts for meaning. There's no point coming up with a system that forces us to deny our innermost needs and yearnings.

Thirdly, our system of meaning must be able to give us strength and courage as we go through our lives, irrespective of what life throws at us. Our system may be all well and good when life is going well, but if it collapses under the weight of suffering, death or failure, then the system is no good. Suffering, death and failure are an inescapable part of life and every system of meaning must be able to cope with that reality. Our system must not collapse at the first faint whiff of a rotting corpse.

Finally, our system of meaning should be a source of joy. It should enrich and enhance not just our life, but the lives of everyone and everything around us.

Spend a bit of time reflecting on these four criteria. You may think of others that you want to include, or perhaps you may think some of the four are less important than others. There is still a lot of work to do on this bank of the creek.

As you can see, declaring the universe meaningless, doesn't get you out from under the hammer. That yearning in your heart won't let you go so easily. You may even be wondering if it's possible to create a system of meaning that fits all those criteria. Well, let me tell you, it is. It's just not easy and it requires a few leaps of faith.

We yearn for meaning in a meaningless universe and this yearning won't go away. It demands that we adhere to a set of pretty stringent characteristics for us to live a meaningful life. Even on this side of the creek, we are not free to chart our own course and still lead a meaningful life.

We'll come back to this side of the creek later but for now, let's jump back across the creek to the undecided bank.

Aristotle: On Persuasion

Before we jump across to the theism side of the creek, let's take a moment to have a look at why people choose which bank to jump to.

About 350 years before Jesus was born, a Greek Philosopher named Aristotle analysed the means by which people become convinced of things. Like Kant, nearly 2000 years later, Aristotle knew that reason alone was seldom enough to convince a person of a certain point of view. For Aristotle, there were three elements that combined to make a person believe what they believed: *logos* (reason or logic), *ethos* (the beliefs and attitudes of those around us, particularly those we regard highly), and *pathos* (what we want to be true.)

So far, this book has been focused almost entirely on *logos*, even though it's clear that reason cannot get us to any definite answer when it comes to meaning in life. But in today's world there are intelligent people who believe all sorts of things that are completely illogical. I've already discussed the fundamentally illogical position of rationalism or scientism. And yet, there are many highly intelligent, articulate humans who hold firmly to that world view and insist that anyone who doesn't agree are wrong.

These people are often given a great deal of respect in our society even though they are wrong. As a result of this, many people are persuaded by them because they are seen to be intelligent or articulate. Most of the people who hold to the rationalist position today do so not because of *logos*, but because of *ethos*. They see someone who is admirable and they get caught up in their belief.

The effect of *ethos* is seen far and wide in our society. Most Christians are not believers because of *logos*. Often their parents were Christians and they were taken to church as children and taught to pray at night before they went to sleep. This was my experience and so even though I'm focusing very much on *logos* in this quest for meaning, I know deep down that my Catholic upbringing has deeply influenced me. Some of my earliest memories are of my parents wrestling with religious ideas. Debating God's mercy and love and trying to make sense of moral conundrums. Has it compromised my ability to think rationally about the issue? Almost certainly.

By the same token, most young people nowadays are not taken to church and are not taught to pray before sleep. Even those who come from nominally Christian homes, live in an environment where God is never mentioned or discussed. Discussions about meaning, and life after death are taboo. Their schools, their friends, their sporting heroes. None of them discuss religious questions. Does this compromise their ability to think rationally about the question of meaning in life? Damn right it does!

You may know quite a few Christians. If most of the Christians you know are bigoted, small minded and judgmental, it wouldn't be surprising to find yourself rejecting their views without even logically exploring their worth. I know personally, that part of the reason why I disagree with evangelical atheists is because I find many of their leading spokesmen (they tend to be mainly men), smug and arrogant. This is another example of *ethos* affecting our beliefs.

I hope, as you are reading this, that you know many wonderful Christians and many wonderful Atheists. Because believe me, the world is full of wonderful people who have many different world views. If you think Atheists are arrogant or greedy, then you haven't met enough of them. Some of the most loving, gentle and humble people I know are Atheists. By the same token, if you think Christians are ignorant, reactionary, bigots, you haven't met enough of them. Some of the finest people who have ever lived are Christians.

Finally, there is *pathos*. I think many of us don't appreciate this element of persuasion enough. What do you want to be true? Some people are naturally drawn to conspiracy theories and minority views. Others want to go with the majority. This tendency will certainly affect which bank of the creek we choose.

At the end of last chapter, I discussed the tension between our desire for freedom and our desire for meaning. Which do you want more? Meaning and purpose in your life or freedom to be the master of your own destiny? Which do you fear more? To be cast adrift in a meaningless universe doomed to die, or to be beholden to some higher Authority that may or may not have your best interests at heart? Scary choice, huh? But don't be afraid. Push on. I promise, the quest is worth it.

All three elements, *logos*, *ethos* and *pathos*, cooperate in our decision about which bank we leap to. To make a sincere choice, we must accept all three elements in our decision and recognise that as we go through our lives, they will all change. There is no right or wrong in the decision you make, there is only integrity versus hypocrisy.

For my part, when I was a child, I had a rudimentary understanding of the *logos* of theism. My family were Catholics and even though church was boring, I never really considered that God wouldn't exist.

When I was a young man, I had a pretty sound understanding of the philosophical arguments, and could see the arguments for both atheism and theism, but my community was all Catholic. I used to say, "My friends, my family and everybody I associate with, are middle class, politically left leaning and Christian". *Ethos* kept me on the Theist bank.

For me now, the arguments against God's existence seem stronger than ever before and there are many people who are either not religious or atheist in my social circle. But, I can't bear to live a meaningless life doomed to death. I lack the courage and strength of Albert Camus and the idea of just making up some meaning for myself seems absurd to me. I am Christian now primarily because of *pathos*.

I have jumped across the creek to the theist bank. I have no idea what sort of a God awaits me. If the attitudes of some Christians are true, I could be in for a very unpleasant time of it when I meet my maker. But so be it. I have nowhere else to go.

Aristotle's three elements of persuasion will reappear often as we journey across the far side of the creek. Because this won't be our first leap. Now come and jump across the creek with me, you may be surprised to find that beyond the leap of faith, the path of reason is waiting.

The Theist Bank : What Can We Know About God?

Now that we've assumed God's existence, reason can be brought into play again. People often say, "it's all faith", as if there is no reason involved in the religious or spiritual quest. This is not true. Faith and reason are not incompatible. You need both faith and reason for this journey.

Let me give you an example, imagine there is a creature living 200m below the surface of the Earth. We don't know if this creature exists or not, but if it did, there are some logical consequences we could propose about this creature, such as its ability to withstand heat, pressure, a low oxygen environment and the kind of energy it might use for survival. In the same way, we don't know if God exists, but there are some logical consequences that would necessarily follow if God did.

Thomas Aquinas' First Cause argument, does not prove the existence of God, but what it shows is that if God exists, then there are some definite qualities that must be associated with Her. These qualities or logical consequences follow from God's existence.

Remember, we are defining God as the source of all meaning. Therefore we can say that if meaning exists, there are some logical conseuences that follow from it's existence. There are three of these logical consequences, Theologians use the words *eternal*, *transcendent* and *immanent* to describe them. Let's take these three things one at a time.

If God exists, God must be eternal

Aquinas says that God is the first cause and thus has no other cause. How can something cause everything else and yet not have a cause itself? Aquinas also states everything that has a beginning has a cause. So God, if God exists, cannot have a beginning. That's why God doesn't have a cause. The word we use to describe this is *eternal*.

Eternal doesn't mean old. It means not subject to time. Many people have a mental image of God as an old man sitting on a cloud. That's not a bad metaphor for children, but it's nowhere near the truth. God is not old. God is *eternal*; not subject to time. "Old" and "eternal" are two very different things. Another way of understanding this is thinking of God as having all Her '*nows*' at once.

Right 'now', I'm sitting at my computer writing this section. It's raining outside. Yesterday, I was out collecting wood for the winter and it was a beautiful autumn day. When I was collecting wood, I was experiencing a different 'now'. Tomorrow is Easter and we'll be gathering around the Easter fire. When I'm standing around that fire, feeling its warmth, I will experience that moment as 'now'. All my 'nows' are stretched out in time from my birth to my death. This is true for all beings that are subject to time.

But God is not subject to time. God's experience of me collecting wood and me writing at my computer and me standing by the fire are all occurring at once. For God, the big bang, the death of Jesus, the dropping of the atomic bomb on Hiroshima, the moment you're reading this word, and the eventual end of the universe are all occurring 'now'.

How can this be? There are a few analogies that help us understand this. A couple of years ago, I wrote a novel. I created a world that's different from ours and created characters that were born, lived and died. My characters experienced their birth, their lives and their deaths as a series of 'nows'. By putting them on the page, I laid out their 'nows' as a series of events throughout the book. My characters experienced the events in order. But, the characters exist within me. I sit on my couch and look at the book on my bookshelf and for me their whole lives are present; every story, every event, all at the same time. I experience all their 'now's' at once.

A similar experience can occur when we reread a book or watch a film. I love Lord of The Rings. When Gandalf falls into the chasm with the Balrog, my heart breaks. When Merry and Eowyn ride off to battle, my heart sings. When Aragorn gives his speech before the black gate, I'm ready to run through a brick wall. And when Sam catches Frodo's hand and says, "Don't you let go," I weep, even though I don't understand why. But I know how this story ends. I shouldn't revisit the emotions over and over again. And yet I do. It's as if, in Lord of the Rings, I have all my 'nows' at once.

> *As a digression, I often used to tell my students not to get caught up in whatever was happening in their life at the moment. Maybe your life is very hard. Maybe you are experiencing terrible grief or suffering. But you must remember that your life is not over. You're only in chapter 2 or maybe chapter 8. The suffering is real, but it will all make sense once the book is finished. You'll close the back cover, stare at the front page again and say, "Wow! What a great story".*

I don't know what will be going on in your life when you read this, my darlings. But remember, your story is not over. You are a character created by the greatest Author of all. Don't worry, your story will be wonderful.

If God exists, God must be transcendent

In the previous section, I have shown that if God exists, God must have no beginning, and no end. God must be eternal. What kind of being is eternal? We can search the universe, look at all the elements, and we cannot find anything that has no beginning and no end. Even light and energy have a beginning. We don't know of anything that is eternal. This leads to a second really important thing we can say about God.

Everything we know and experience has a beginning, has a cause and is subject to time. However, if God is the first cause, She has no beginning and is not subject to time. Therefore She must be completely different to everything else we know and experience. This leads to the second claim we can make. God is *transcendent*. This means that God is utterly beyond human experience and understanding. God is the eternal, uncaused cause.

If God exists, God must be fundamentally different from everything else in the universe. One way to think of this is that existence is like a great chain. A great chain of being, where each link in the chain is held up by the link above it. This chain stretches from you to me, and up through the eons to the first proto-creature wriggling in the primordial soup. We all share this common condition of being caused by something that came before us. God must be completely different from all the links of the chain because God is uncaused. God is like a post, driven into the ground from which the chain hangs. The post and the ground are completely transcendent compared to the links in the chain.

If God exists, God must be immanent

There is a third really important consequence from the first cause argument. This is the idea that even though God must be transcendent, She must also be *immanent*. In simple terms, this means "God is everywhere."

When I was in primary school, we used to tell a joke...

> *"Little Johnny was pushing his billy cart up the hill. As he was going, he was swearing and kicking at it, "Get up the hill, you bloody shit of a thing!"*
>
> *Father O'Grady was passing and saw him behaving this way. "Now, Johnny, don't swear. God can hear you. God is everywhere!"*
>
> *Johnny looked up in amazement. "God is everywhere?!"*
>
> *"Oh yes," said the priest, pleased to have had an impact on the boy.*
>
> *"Is God in me?"*
>
> *"Oh most certainly, Johnny."*
>
> *"Is God in my billy cart?"*
>
> *Father O'Grady smiled. "Yes, Johnny. God is everywhere. Even in your billy cart."*
>
> *Johnny straightened himself to his full height, stared at the priest with outrage in his eyes and said, "Then why doesn't the bastard he get out of my fucken' billy cart and help me push it!"*

Johnny didn't understand the Theological concept of the immanence of God but it's an essential part of any understanding of God. If God exists, She must be immanent. How can this be?

If God is the *first* cause, then there could be no primal matter that existed before creation. Theologians use the phase, "God brought everything into existence from nothing (*ex nihilo*)". If this is the case, then the only 'stuff' that God could use to create the universe must have been within God.

God created the universe out of Herself. It's not like the person who carved the sentence on the rock face, who found the rock, pre-made. It's more like a chicken who lays an egg. When my children were newborn babies, I remember staring at them as they were being breast fed and marveling that every part of their bodies came out of the body of their mother. It's an extraordinary thing. Even though these children are now their own person, their mother's essence was impregnated within them in a way that mine was not. (Motherhood really is a wonderful thing! It seems to me that Jesus made a mistake to use Father as a metaphor for God. It should have been Mother).

If God created the universe out of Herself, then there must be traces, or elements of God's being shot through the finite universe. This is really important, because without these traces, we would have no hope of getting anywhere near the mind of God and our quest for meaning would fail. There must be an infinite reality hiding within the finite universe. We just have to find it.

But, be careful. When we say God is immanent, we don't mean that God is within the universe. We mean the Universe is within God. There's an old story, I used to tell my students.

> *Two young fish were swimming in the sea and they came upon and older fish.*

> *"How's the water, boys?" said the old fish, and then swam on without waiting for an answer.*
>
> *The two young fish looked at each other in confusion. "What's water?" they said.*

If we are so immersed in something that there is nowhere where it 'is not', then that 'thing' can become invisible. St Paul says that "we live, move, and have our being" in God. It's as if the universe is a sponge floating in the ocean. The water is everywhere, and it permeates and surrounds the sponge.

It's like the characters in my book. I created them, and fundamentally, they exist entirely within my mind. I created them from my own life experiences and personality traits, my very essence is shot through every aspect of that book but my characters have no way of knowing I exist.

It's very important to understand these three concepts. Despite the fact that we cannot know if God exists or not, we can say with certainty that *if* God exists, God *must be* eternal, transcendent and immanent. Amazingly, these are rocks of certainty in a river of uncertainty. We will keep coming back to these three concepts repeatedly as we continue our quest because the implications of these three concepts are very wide reaching.

Next chapter we will begin to consider the implications of God's transcendence and discuss the vital role of symbols and symbolic language in our quest for meaning.

5

Symbolic Language

Analogy, Metaphor and Symbol

Jesuit theologian Roger Haight says Christians declare God to be transcendent and then completely disregard this concept for the rest of our lives. But once we accept the transcendence of God, there are some very serious consequences that must be taken into account at every step of our quest for meaning. One of the most important is, that we can only access God (ie. meaning: remember we've defined God as the source of meaning) through analogy, metaphor and symbol.

If God is transcendent, then we must accept that nothing we say about God is perfectly true. God is beyond our understanding so any image we have in our minds, any thought we have about God, is not God. We must be very careful never to confuse our mental image of God with God Herself. Whenever we think or talk about God, we must remain humble. We are playing way out of our league.

Based on the necessary transcendence of God, Thomas Aquinas developed the Doctrine of Analogy. Because God is transcendent, anything we say about God must be a little bit wrong (Aquinas used the term "*imperfect*"). For Aquinas, then, the only way we can describe God is through analogy and metaphor. You've probably already noticed that every time I've tried to talk about God, I've resorted to analogy and metaphor. It's impossible to do anything else because all the words in our language are based on things in the universe. Finite things that have a beginning and a cause and are subject to time. Every word we use to describe God, then, is not quite right.

For example, when we say "God is good". The word "good" refers to our human concept of goodness. My mum was good to me; I had a good dinner last night – these are finite, not eternal beings. When I say, "God is good", I'm using a word created in the finite universe, to describe something transcendent. It's as if we are limited only to words that describe the chain, as we try to describe the post and the ground. We're not going to get very far. So everything we say about God is either analogy or metaphor, and we need to keep this in our minds at all times and not take our words too literally.

There are several types of language that we can use to try to describe God, meaning and the spiritual life. The first is, as I've said, analogy ('God is like'). The second is metaphor. Metaphor is very similar to analogy but we don't bother to say 'like' or 'as if'. I can say that a young footballer "Played like a tiger that day" (analogy). Or I could say, "He was tiger on the field that day" (metaphor). The metaphor does not make him an actual tiger. They are both making the same point but to my mind, the second one has slightly more power.

By and large we are pretty good at recognising the limits of an analogy, but we are terrible at recognising the limits of a metaphor. It would be silly for someone to say that the young footballer was not a very good player because he doesn't have claws and yellow and black stripes. When I was teaching, one my most common responses to my students' questions was, "metaphor metaphor metaphor!" Everything we say about God is a metaphor.

The third type of language we use about God is *symbolic*. A symbol is an object that makes a transcendent reality present and known. Here are a couple of examples:

In the front garden of my house in Faygate Court, there is a Hibiscus tree. My mum planted it while my daughter Emily was sick. The little tree struggled to survive. Its leaves withered and curled. It seemed to be always dry and there was no new growth. It seemed certain to die, but Mum never gave up watering, tending, caring. Eventually, it slowly began to put forth new leaves. The plant gained colour and began to thrive. Mum declared it, "the Emily tree." She would show Em the tree and tell her how she too would one day thrive.

Emily and Mum are long dead, but the tree is still thriving and putting forth beautiful red flowers every summer. For me, that tree will always be a symbol of my mum and my daughter. When it puts forth its flowers it somehow makes them present to me.

When I was a kid my grandmother used to come and stay with us every few months. She would always use the same white mug to make her tea. She was pretty slack at washing it and she drank a lot of tea. As a result, the mug was stained sepia on the inside. It looked pretty gross and nobody ever drank from it. We called it, 'Granny's cup'.

After my granny died, the cup stayed in Mum and Dad's cupboard and nobody used it.

When I moved out of home a few years later, I took Granny's cup with me. Granny's cup became mine.

I was never very close to Granny, but it felt good sharing a cup with her. My flatmates knew the story and they too called it 'Granny's cup'.

One day, Granny's cup was soaking in the sink waiting to be washed (I'm pretty slack at washing dishes too). One of the blokes who was sharing my flat, dropped his plate into the sink carelessly, and the cup broke. There was a terrible moment of grief as I realised that I had lost something more than just a cup.

The thing about symbols is that they are really powerful. They can make transcendent things present. But nothing lasts forever. Eventually, the Emily tree will die. All the mementos and sentimental things I have in my cupboard will perish. They are symbols of a transcendent reality. But they are not the reality itself.

Sometimes, events or stories can become symbols. The previous paragraphs contain two symbolic stories. A symbolic story is a powerful way of communicating things that are beyond words. A shared set of symbols, particularly symbolic stories, are really important in binding a group of people together.

Stories, metaphors and analogies are all part of what we call *symbolic language*. Christians are bound together by a shared symbolic language. Our interpretation of these things can often differ wildly and this causes confusion and tension, but this is the only language we have to express meaning.

Because symbols can mean different things to different people, symbols live and die within culture. If someone didn't know what a tiger was, describing a football player as a tiger on the football field would be meaningless. Keep this in mind because a lot of religious beliefs and practices are symbols from different times and different cultures. The symbols created by people of the past may not hold the same meaning for us as it did for them.

Symbolic language can't fully express the transcendent reality it makes present. The symbols are all necessarily imperfect because they are part of the finite universe. Each symbol, metaphor, story or analogy is a like a spotlight shining on a statue in the night. Each light shines from a different direction. It illuminates some parts of the statue but casts another part into shadow. Even using all the spotlights, we can never see the whole statue at once because no matter where we stand, there is always some part of the statue which is hidden.

Come with me now, as I take you around the statue shining different spotlights at different aspects. I can't show you the whole statue, but I can give you a language, some mental models to use in your thinking, and a dim outline that will help you to find the meaning that you seek.

Spiritual Experiences: encounters with Meaning

You could be forgiven at this point for thinking that our quest for meaning is futile. If God is the source of ultimate meaning, and God must be transcendent and eternal, then our quest is lost. Meaning might as well be on the far side of the galaxy. We can never find it.

But fortunately for us, God, the source of all meaning, is also immanent. This means that She is everywhere, as close to us as the very air we breathe. All we have to do is open ourselves and God (the source of meaning) is there. Throughout history, countless people from all the cultures, races and religions of the world have done just that and encountered God.

We use many different terms to name these encounters, but by and large, the catch-all descriptor is *'spiritual experiences'*. Spiritual experiences come in all different shapes and sizes. A shepherd sees a bush on fire while walking in the wilderness. A woman comes to a well to draw water. Someone is sitting under a tree. Another person is preparing to lead his troops into battle. Suddenly, usually unexpectedly, they encounter *Something*.

Each encounter occurs under different circumstances and those who experience them use different words to describe them. But many of those who have studied these encounters have concluded these encounters have lots in common. So much so, that many Catholic theologians believe that each spiritual experience is in fact an encounter with a single source of meaning. It's as if several people are in a dark room and a curtain is torn away, revealing a window they never knew was there. Suddenly sunlight floods the room affecting all those inside. Each person in the room may be doing something different and experience the light flooding differently. But it's only one window, and one source of light.

My first experience of God was when I was about 12 years old. It was my first term in year seven. Every Wednesday afternoon, the whole year level would be taken to the lecture theatre and we would be shown a series of films based on stories from the Old Testament. Abraham, Isaac, Jacob – we went through them all. I used to enjoy it. I had a vague knowledge of the stories but it was a different experience seeing them acted out. The people in these stories may have dressed differently to me, but they were like me. They weren't holy or even particularly nice, but their lives were interesting.

When Joshua sacked the city of Jericho I was appalled, but I figured it was war and people do terrible things in war. So I let it pass. We eventually got to the story of Elijah and the prophets of Baal. Elijah orders all the prophets of the Baal to be killed because they didn't believe in the 'One True God'. That was too much for me. I went home from school with my emotions swirling. What sort of a God orders people to be killed in cold blood just because they believe in a different religion? It was unthinkable.

That night, as I lay in bed, I remembered that Abraham, Isaac, Jacob and all those people in the bible films spoke freely and honestly to God. I tentatively reached out with my mind and offered a shy prayer. "Excuse me, I'd like to talk to God, please." I thought about praying to Jesus but then, I wasn't sure if Christianity was true and I didn't want to risk praying to the wrong God. Also, I had a complaint. I didn't want to waste time with the second in command, I wanted to take it to the top.

I remember not wanting to offend anyone 'up there' so I said, "I'm sorry Jesus, I'm not saying I don't believe in you, I'd just like to talk to your Father, if that's okay."

I assumed that the connection to God had been made and then began my complaint. I don't remember exactly what I said but as I spoke, I got more and more angry, ranting and raving about the injustice of it all and the fact that the prophets of Baal were defenseless and had done nothing wrong. (Keep in mind, I was speaking in my mind, not out loud. I might have been a weird kid but I wasn't crazy!)

Suddenly, it was as if something exploded in my chest. I can't explain it in words. I felt this burning in my heart. Like how you feel when someone you love, tells you that they love you. But on steroids. I remember being stunned into silence. Then, the prophets of Baal, the people of Jericho, Joshua, Elijah and all the others disappeared from view. It was as if God had stepped out of heaven into my room and told me that She loved me.

I was completely awestruck by what was happening. I remember putting my hands over my mouth in amazement, at one level finding it hard to believe that this was happening to me but at another, knowing with a certainty beyond reason that my life was never going to be the same again.

I don't remember how long I kept my experience secret, but eventually I tried to talk about it to my mum. It must have been the weekend because I remember it was daylight, and she was in the kitchen and not wearing her work clothes.

"Mum," I began, "have you ever felt like God was right...there." Even as I said the words, I knew I was not going to be able to tell her what it felt like.

She put down her tea towel and looked at me very seriously. "When I was in the convent, I felt very close to God." Mum did part of her high schooling in a boarding school run by nuns. She always called it 'the convent'. *"I remember at the end of term, travelling home on the train and I could see the monstrance from the altar in my minod's eye and I felt,"* she put her hand to her chest, her voice heavy with emotion, *"so close Him."*

I tried not to let the disappointment show on my face. I could tell from the way she spoke that Mum felt this deeply, but to my 12-year-old mind, a church altar with a golden monstrance had nothing to do with the extraordinary experience I had in my room.

What I didn't understand then was that we were both struggling to find words to describe an experience that was beyond words. I was concentrating on her words, instead of trying to understand her experience.

Characteristics of Spiritual Experiences

There are many, many people who have had similar (or different) encounters but they are all encounters with the Transcendent One. These encounters are as varied as the people who experienced them. In fact, all the religious traditions in human history are based on encounters with the ultimate source of meaning, the one that Christians call God.

These experiences are so common that Theologians have studied them and come up with a few general characteristics that they all share.

Firstly, all these experiences are *mediated*. Whether it's a sunset, a golden statue or a burning bush, something finite or concrete is always central to the religious experience. Sometimes it's a book or a conversation or maybe an encounter with another person. Whatever the circumstances of a religious experience, there is always some natural or finite reality that makes the transcendent present and known.

Even my experience of praying in my bed when I was 12 was entirely mediated through my mind and my body. I was thinking, synapses in my brain were going off, chemicals and hormones were being generated and my metabolism reacted to them. Everything I experienced was completely embedded in my finite, human situation in a specific place and time.

For years after, I would often wonder if I had really encountered God that night, or if it had just been my mind whipping me up into some sort of delusional state. Now I believe that it was both. I encountered the transcendent ground and horizon of all being mediated through my finite body and mind.

Experiences are not natural or supernatural, they are all natural, but through some of them we encounter a deeper presence, a deeper sense of meaning. So there is no point trying to explain away or prove a miraculous source for any of these experiences. Whether our contemporary science can explain the experience or not is irrelevant. There are some things that can be explained by our contemporary science and there are some things that can't. Almost everything can be partially explained by our contemporary science but that doesn't alter the significance of the experience. It's not the medium that counts, but the transcendence that is being mediated.

The second characteristic of these spiritual experiences is that they are *apophatic*. This means that humans do not have language to express them. We can talk about the mediating parts of the experience, the sunlight dancing through the leaves, or the hand reaching out to touch a face, but when it comes to the transcendent reality that has been mediated, our words fail. If you go back and read the way I described my experience and the way my mum described hers, you'll see that we were both forced into metaphor and analogy because once we moved beyond the mundane, we had no words to describe the encounter. This is a really important insight. Since all spiritual experiences are apophatic, no account of a spiritual experience is 100% accurate. Like Aquinas' doctrine of analogy, we are forced to resort to metaphor and analogy, or draw on shared stories to dimly hint at an experience that is beyond words.

There is also a third characteristic. Even though these experiences cannot be described, once we've had one, we want to talk about it. This is called *cataphatic*. We experience something that turns our world upside down and we want to share it with others. But we can't find the words, so we often find ourselves talking about it over and over, trying vainly to communicate the noncommunicable.

This is very common in life even outside of spiritual experiences. When a person falls in love, they often find themselves talking about the object of their love. They tell stories about the person they are in love with or draw comparisons between this person and others. When I have been in this situation, I've often had to will myself to keep silent because I know how boring it is for the people who have to listen. No matter how much the lover talks, the transcendent experience of love cannot be transferred to another.

Interestingly, this aspect of romantic love is different from spiritual experiences. It's quite common for a person to experience the transcendent while hearing another person's account of their own spiritual experience. But it's important to remember that when this happens, the spiritual experience is unique to the person receiving it. When Moses saw a burning bush and rushed back to camp to tell his brother, Aaron, Aaron's experience of the divine was not mediated by the burning bush. It was mediated by Moses telling him about it.

This leaves us in the same situation we were in last chapter. Spiritual experiences are encounters through which transcendent reality is made present and known. We talk about them, because they are cataphatic, but we cannot fully express them because they are apophatic. So, we are forced to resort to stories, metaphors or analogies. They too are a kind of a spotlight shining on the mysterious statue which is the ultimate source of meaning.

If we jump back to the atheist bank of the creek, we could say that all these spiritual experiences are just our own mind imposing patterns of meaning on an otherwise random or fundamentally meaningless phenomenon. Like when we look into the sky and see the shape of a bunny rabbit in the clouds. The clouds are just water vapour, randomly arranging themselves under the forces of gravity and wind. The bunny is a fabrication of our own mind, our human yearning for meaning and pattern making.

But from the theist bank of the creek, it actually makes perfect sense. An immanent, transcendent God must be present in every aspect of finite reality. If God exists, She must be pulsating through every fibre of the universe, in the same way as an author is intimately present in every scene in his novel. Our yearning for meaning is not an aberration. We are not tragically thrown into a meaningless universe beset with an irrational longing. The universe is fully charged with meaning and purpose. That's why we yearn for it. That yearning has been placed in our hearts to enable us to see the meaning that is always there.

The question is not "How do we explain these encounters with God?" it's "How do we explain why we don't have them all the time?" We are like the two young fish I talked about last chapter, yearning for an experience of water.

6

Scripture and Tradition

The catholic Conversation

There is a common misconception in contemporary society that Religion, Spirituality and the quest for meaning is purely an individual matter. If you ask an adult a question on these matters you may well receive the response, "these things are personal". There is no doubt that those who say this often are driven by a worthwhile desire to allow people freedom of worship and there is a deep truth in what they say. We can't blindly adopt another person's system of meaning or impose one person's system on another. To truly find meaning in life, we must make the quest ourselves and integrate the insights into our own lives. In this sense, the quest for meaning is certainly personal. You must do the work and only you can do it.

But we cannot claim that the quest is *only* personal. You didn't pop into existence out of nothing. You were born into a family, that belonged to a society that embraced a culture that arose out of historical circumstances. And all of this is embedded deeply in the biosphere of a small blue-green planet in an unremarkable galaxy in a vast universe. Everything you experience, everything you think, everything you are, occurs within those constraints. I am writing this book as if you and I were on a journey alone in a disembodied universe. But it's not like that at all. Everything I'm telling you, all the twists and turns of the path, have been constructed by those who have gone before us.

An historian by the name of Eamon Duffy wrote, *"Catholicism is a conversation crossing continents and cultures, stretching backwards and forwards in time"*. But this is not only true of Catholicism, the entire human quest for meaning is a such a conversation. Maybe hundreds of thousands of years ago someone watched the sun rise from the mouth of their cave, felt a stirring in their deepest heart and wondered, "what does this all mean?" From that profound first moment until the moment you are reading this sentence, the human race has been engaged in a complex conversation. Together we have searched for meaning and expressed that meaning through many different Religious Traditions. No one has ever made the journey alone. You are never alone. Even as you read this paragraph, you are surrounded by 'a vast cloud of witnesses'. People who have gone before you and people who are yet to be born. We're all on this journey together.

The word *catholic* means "according to the whole" or "universal". At it's best Catholicism includes everybody. It is a tragedy that in our generation, 'Catholic' has become a label that differentiates one group of people from another. That was not meant to be the case. Everyone is part of the great symphony of life. We are all participants in the one conversation. Not a Catholic conversation that only includes people who are part of the Roman Catholic Church, but a *catholic* one. A conversation that includes every religion and every human being.

Most of those who say there is no meaning in life, have never seriously searched for it. It's very important to realise that the vast majority of those who searched for meaning, found it. The meaning they discovered didn't lend itself to simple words because it was apophatic, but they tried to communicate their insights because meaning, when found, is cataphatic. Humans have always used stories, symbols, images, myths and rituals, to share our imperfect insights.

The conversation that probably began in an African cave 300,000 years ago still echoes down the ages. As the participants come and go, they leave a mark on the conversation and this whole edifice is handed down as the generations of humanity come and go. This is what the word *"tradition"* means. Literally, "that which is handed on". Each generation hands on its knowledge and insights to the next. And you, in your turn, will hand it on to those who will come after you. That tradition is not a collection of separate stories or events. It is one encounter with the ultimate source of meaning. One Great Tradition.

The Bible: Take it seriously, not Literally

Let's take what we've discovered about spiritual experiences and the Great Tradition and apply them to the Bible and its role in our quest for meaning. What is The Bible? What is it not? Why does it matter?

In the world today, we are drowning in a sea of ignorant certainty. Since the start of the 20th century, the popular discussion on The Bible has been dominated by two schools of thought.

The first is called *Fundamentalism*. This is the belief that The Bible is a book containing the literal words of God. From this perspective, everything stated in The Bible is absolutely and literally true. There are no internal contradictions and no mistakes of any kind. Fundamentalists believe the Bible is religiously, historically, scientifically true. So every part of The Bible can be used as a blueprint for how we live our lives, run our societies, and understand our science. This has led people to accept some pretty outlandish ideas. For example, beliefs like the world being made in 6 days, dinosaurs living at the same time as humans, women shouldn't have the same rights as men and some even argue (based on The Bible) that the world is flat.

In reaction to this, an opposing force has arisen which claims the Bible is nothing more than a document of Bronze Age morality. It is irrelevant to us, full of crazy stories and meaningless rules. It has sexism, racism, war and slavery embedded in it, and it is the single best argument that Christianity is bullshit.

Both these positions share a common assumption. That the Bible claims to be the inerrant words of God. I must confess a bias here. If I were to accept that fundamental assumption, then I too would be forced to agree with the atheist position. It's not just the inconsistencies in the Bible. There is racism, sexism, and scientific ignorance shot through nearly every page. How can a person believe that it's literally the words of God? But the Bible is not just one book and it is not the words of God. The Bible was written by people, just like you and me. They weren't secretaries who took down God's words as She dictated them. They were people trying to write things that they thought were valuable.

My year 7's and 8's would fight me on this and we'd have a lot of fun arguing it out. Sometimes I used to get parents ringing up to complain as well. When it comes to Religious Education, fundamentalism is a pain in the arse.

Let's take this step by step. Firstly, The Bible is not a book. It's a library. We carry it around in a single volume, with a front and back cover and many pages in between. This appearance often leads us to misunderstand what it really is. It is actually a small library. That's why we talk about the "books of The Bible". Each book in The Bible has been written by a different person (often several different people) at a different time and with a different purpose.

Asking "is The Bible true?" is like asking, "is the library true?" It depends on what sort of truth you're talking about and what part of the library you're investigating. In your local library, there are history books, science books, fiction, poetry, opinion pieces. They don't all agree. The history books often contain scientific errors and the science books often contain historical errors. And the poetry! Why on earth would you try to learn science by studying poetry? What about novels? Imagine trying to learn science by studying Star Wars, or history by studying The Lord of the Rings, or biology by studying The Chronicles of Narnia. The kids in my classes would enjoy this train of thought. We'd often get distracted imagining what kind of ridiculous ideas we'd come up with if we took our favourite movies and books literally (one of my favourites was equipping the Australian army with light sabres).

In the same way, The Bible has books of history, philosophy, poetry, fiction, biographies, old letters and myth. They are all really important parts of the library. But to understand it, we've got to understand who wrote it, when they wrote it, and why they wrote it.

How the Bible was written

When we consider how the Bible came to exist, there are four steps that need to be considered.

Firstly: someone has a spiritual experience. At the heart of every book of The Bible is a mediated, apophatic spiritual experience. Someone's donkey refuses to go down a certain road, someone else hears a story of courage when facing overwhelming odds, another person meets a stranger walking through a garden. Some events seem ordinary while others seem to defy logical explanation. But it's not the events that are important, it's the apophatic encounter with the transcendent Other that makes itself present through them.

Secondly: That experience was so profound, that they felt compelled to talk about it. But it can't be expressed in words. So they must resort to symbolic language; story, metaphor, analogy, symbol to get the story across. This means, you can't take the words of the Bible literally. They are symbolic language. They are stories, metaphors and analogies, trying to communicate something which is beyond words.

Thirdly: Sometimes, when the stories are told, the listeners also have spiritual experiences. The listeners then pass their stories on, But when they do, they are trying to share their own apophatic encounter not than the original experience.

Finally: sometimes after hundreds of years, those stories are written down. In ancient times, writing a book cost a lot of time and resources. It was not done lightly. The people who wrote the books were also trying to communicate their apophatic spiritual experience and they too used symbolic language.

For some of the books, getting the history right was very important, but only in so far as communicating the spiritual truth behind the story. In other books, the authors embedded the scientific understanding of their day within the text. They weren't in the least bit interested in the history or the science. They were all trying to tell a story with a deeper meaning. So we can't assume that what the Bible says about science and history is 100% correct. That's not the point of the writings.

When you hold a Bible in your hand, you are holding the hearts, dreams and yearnings of countless people. The ones who first experienced the events, the ones who passed the stories on and the ones who wrote the stories down. Often ordinary people, just like you and me. They weren't morally perfect or supremely intelligent. They were products of their society and their upbringing, just like we are products of ours. Many of them were raised in cultures that were racist, sexist or ignorant of science and history. That's why there are so many examples of racism, sexism and ignorance in the Bible.

But that's not why we hold onto this library. These are the accounts of others who were searching for meaning in their lives. Each of them experienced the transcendent God that gave their life meaning, and they tried to pass that experience on to you. Some people sacrificed their lives so that you would have this book, because they believed that life has meaning and that you deserved to know it.

The Word of God, not the Words of God.

My students would often get uncomfortable when I'd tell them that the Bible is not the words of God. They'd say "But they call it the Word of God in church", or a similar argument. That would be my opening to explore how mainstream Christians understand The Bible as the *Word* of God, not the *words* of God. It's a big, big difference.

These encounters are not separate and unrelated. Each spiritual experience is part of one encounter, one *Word* spoken from transcendence to the hungry human heart. A Christian would say, "One word of God" not many words of God.

So all humanity's spiritual experiences are encounters with one single source of meaning. All our stories, symbols and rituals are part of one Great Tradition that tries to hand on this meaning. Everything written in the Bible is an attempt to hand on this amazing encounter with the ultimate source of meaning. This is what Christians mean when they talk about the Bible being "The Word of God'. I will say more about this One Word later.

We are all little fish, swimming in a great ocean. Every now and then one of us discovers that we are immersed in water and we try to share it with others. This little book you're reading today, is my feeble attempt to show you the water that you're swimming in. But even though there are many fish, there is only one ocean. There is only one great encounter with the ultimate source of meaning, the one word of God. This is what Catholics call the Great Tradition. We each experience it in our own way and we all try to hand it on, because it's so wonderful that we don't want you to miss out.

The Bible is a collection of books written and collected by many people to try to give us an encounter with this great source of meaning. That's why Catholics take the Bible seriously, but we don't take it literally.

7

Jesus Of Nazareth

Jesus: Historical Reality or Fantasy

On retreats, we would use this poem to introduce Jesus:

> *He was born in an obscure village*
> *The child of a peasant woman*
> *He grew up in another obscure village*
> *Where he worked in a carpenter shop*
> *Until he was thirty*
> *He never wrote a book*
> *He never held an office*
> *He never went to college*
> *He never visited a big city*
> *He never travelled more than two hundred miles*
> *From the place where he was born*
> *He did none of the things usually associated with greatness*

He had no credentials but himself
He was only thirty three
His friends ran away
One of them denied him
He was turned over to his enemies
And went through the mockery of a trial
He was nailed to a cross between two thieves
While dying, his executioners gambled for his clothing
The only property he had on earth
When he was dead he was laid in a borrowed grave
Through the pity of a friend.
Nineteen centuries have come and gone
And today Jesus is the central figure of the human race
And the leader of mankind's progress
All the armies that have ever marched
All the navies that have ever sailed
All the parliaments that have ever sat
All the kings that ever reigned put together
Have not affected the life of mankind on earth
As powerfully as that one solitary life
  Dr James Allan © 1926.

The conclusion of the poem is contentious, but not unarguable. If we were to discuss which historical character has had the most profound effect on human history, Jesus of Nazareth certainly would be mentioned.

The power of his life is not just tied to his brilliant storytelling, insightful teaching or inspiring poetry. Somehow, through encountering the man and hearing the story of his life, countless people have experienced an apophatic spiritual experience. Somehow (and I'm not trying to be obtuse here, I really don't understand how), encountering Jesus of Nazareth, either in person or through his story, seems to give many people a profound insight into the nature of God and the meaning and purpose of their lives. That was certainly the case for me.

The earliest sources about the life of Jesus of Nazareth are contained in the books of the New Testament. These are drawn from six sources; the four gospels (Mark, Matthew, Luke and John), a collection of sayings which scholars call Q, and the letters of Paul of Tarsus. Matthew and Luke used Q as a source for their books but they each accessed other information as well. Scholars disagree on when these sources were created but there seems to be general consensus that they were all written between 50 AD and 110 AD. That's about 25 to 85 years after the death of Jesus.

To a contemporary mind, that may sound like a long time ago, but in the ancient world, it was not unusual for there to be a long gap between historical events and the written accounts of them. The ancients were mistrustful of written texts, because anyone can make up some rubbish and write it down. For them, the most reliable source of information was a face to face, eyewitness account. And failing that, a face to face account from a non-eyewitness.

This is hard for us to get our heads around because we live in a society where books are printed and bound. Our books have a special authority conveyed upon them by virtue of being published. In the ancient world, books were more like a Reddit thread in our time (I don't know whether there'll still be

Reddit threads when you read this). Because books were handwritten, they could have been written by anyone who had a quill and piece of parchment. There was no way of knowing who wrote them. Whereas, a face to face account enabled a listener to judge the person's mannerisms and facial expressions and therefore get a much better idea of whether or not they were telling the truth.

Many people who have not studied ancient history deeply have leapt to the conclusion that because these sources were written so long after the death of Jesus, they are of no historical value, or at worst, some even claim that Jesus never existed and was merely a fictional creation. A lot of intelligent, well-respected people make this claim, and a lot of people believe them. But they are wrong. There's not a single scholar who specialises in that time period who argues that Jesus never existed.

In addition, there are non-Christian sources from the early years, such as Josephus, Tacitus and Pliny, who all reference Jesus of Nazareth. There is not a single ancient text that claims that Jesus of Nazareth was not an actual historical person.

What can we find out about the life of Jesus?

The common misunderstanding about The Bible often leads us to underestimate the power of the six, New Testament sources. As I mentioned in the previous chapter, we tend to think of The Bible as a single book. We don't think of these six accounts as independent, because 'they are all part of the Bible.' But that's like saying I don't believe the Norman conquest of Britain occurred, because the only books that discuss it are in the library. We have six independent accounts that discuss the life and teaching of Jesus of Nazareth. Sometimes they agree with each other, other times they disagree, and this enables us to get a surprisingly clear picture of the bare bones of Jesus' life.

Scholars of New Testament history can establish a pretty good outline of Jesus' life, by using a few simple and logical rules.

Rule one: The more sources that mention an event in Jesus' life, the more likely it is that the event occurred. If one source contradicts another, then they put the event in the doubtful box.

Rule two: Then they ask, does the event depicted in the source embarrass the author or weaken their general argument? If that's the case, then the event is more likely to be true than not true.

If I tell you two stories. One in which I seem like a hero, and another in which I seem like an idiot, which story is more likely true? I'm not going to make up a story that makes me look bad. I'm much more likely to make one up that makes me look like a hero. Therefore New Testament stories that show Jesus as weak or confused are more believable than stories where he is confident and powerful. Stories that show his followers (the leaders of the Christian community) as greedy or stupid, are more believable than stories that show them as brave or wise.

Finally, rule three: We each have our own literary voice. I have a certain way of writing and if you read enough of what I write, you'd soon be able to instinctively know when you're reading a letter from me. In the same way, scholars are able to analyse the sentence structure and language of the various sayings in the New Testament and sort out the different literary voices within the sources. Because of this, they are able to claim that many (but not all) of the teachings attributed to Jesus seem to come from one source. A single Jewish person.

Based on these three rules, we can be confident that Jesus was a Jewish teacher from Galilee who fell foul of the Religious and Political authorities of his day and was crucified in Jerusalem some time around 30 AD.

We can be pretty confident about a lot more than that but I'm not going to pursue the details of Jesus' life. I want to move on to what Jesus taught, because his teachings are an important spotlight that shines on the mysterious statue we call 'the meaning of life'.

The Teaching of Jesus

The Gospels are full of sayings, stories and teachings attributed to Jesus, and I'm not going to go into them in great detail. Hopefully, you have a New Testament somewhere in your house or in your local library and you can read them for yourself. In this section, I want to focus on what Jesus taught about the meaning and purpose of human life. This broadly comes down to four basic concepts:
  i) our identity
  ii) our purpose and destiny
  iii) the nature of God (the source of all meaning)
  iv) how to live a joyful, meaningful life

i) Our Identity

Let's start with identity. All gospel sources agree that Jesus' public life began when he was baptised by John the Baptist on the banks of the Jordan river. Either at the moment of baptism or directly after (the sources differ), Jesus had a profound, apophatic spiritual experience that completely transformed his life. Jesus experienced, "the heavens opening and the Holy Spirit descending upon him and he heard a voice from heaven saying, *'You are my beloved Son, in whom I am well pleased.'*" Mark Chapter 1. 10-11.
(Remember the only way to describe apophatic experiences is through symbolic language, so don't take this literally).

When we unpack the symbolic language of the above quote, we rapidly get to the absolute heart of Jesus' spiritual insight. He experienced God as a loving father, giving him his identity, i.e., "You are my beloved Son".

Now, it's very important that we let Jesus interpret his spiritual experience and not impose some church dogma onto it. There is no evidence that Jesus ever saw his experience as being only applicable to himself. If you read the earliest Gospels of Mark, Matthew and Luke (John is a special case) it's clear that Jesus did not see himself as the unique son of God. He consistently teaches that we are all sons and daughters of God. For Jesus, his spiritual experience was relevant to everybody. Our identity is that we are all beloved children of the one transcendent, eternal God.

If you've been raised in a mainstream Christian culture, you may shrug your shoulders at this. Two thousand years of repetition have robbed the statement of its radicalism. Most of my students simply took it for granted. They would say, "Yes. We're children of God, but what's the meaning of life?" But being children of God is the meaning of our life. In that one statement we are told who we are, what we are meant to do and what we are destined to become. We just don't join the dots because Jesus is too radical for us.

ii) Our Purpose and our destiny

In rural first century Palestine, children didn't choose a career from a wide variety of options. If your father was a carpenter or a fisherman, then so were you. If Jesus tells us that our Father is God, then guess what he expected us to be when we grow up? This seems overwhelming, doesn't it? I can't even organise a vegetable garden, how am I supposed to be like God? But according to Jesus, it's not as difficult as it first appears.

This leads us to the second important part of Jesus' teaching; our purpose and our destiny. Looking at the metaphor of childhood from a different angle, puppies grow up to be dogs, kittens grow up to be cats. Children grow up to be like their parents. It's not that puppies have to study barking and stick chasing before they can achieve 'doghood'. There is an intrinsic growth that occurs in a puppy that leads it to become a dog. Jesus described this as *the Reign of God*. God is present in the world and ultimately in absolute control of what's happening. We just have to trust God and it will happen.

According to Jesus, the Reign of God is not just limited to us as individuals, there is a whole social, political and economic system associated with it. There is no hierarchy among children of God. No one is supposed to "lord it over anybody else" Matt 20:25. If we are all children of God, then our fellow humans are our brothers and sisters and they deserve our love and respect, because they are also beloved children of God.

So, Jesus taught that not only do we have a job to do (being God), but we have a natural tendency to grow into that state, and an inherent dignity that comes from our status. I used to tell my students, "If you see an old drunk guy lying in a gutter, remember, he is a son of the living God, made in the image and likeness of God and destined to share fully in the divine life."

iii) The Nature of God

But what does it mean to become like God? I mean, what's the job description? So far all we know about God is:

i) by definition, She is the source of all meaning. And

ii) if She exists. She must be eternal, immanent and transcendent.

How on earth are we supposed to be that? This leads us to the third aspect of Jesus' teaching. The nature of God.

Jesus spent a lot of time describing God. Using parables, metaphors, analogies and all sorts of other forms of symbolic language, Jesus taught the that the most important element of God was Love. God loves everybody. For example:

"You must be like perfect as your Father is perfect... who sends his sun to shine on both the good and the evil" (Matthew 5: 44-48).

God's love is not just limited to humans,
"Are not two sparrows sold for a penny? Yet not one of them falls to the ground without your Father's care" (Matthew 10:29).

For Jesus, God is a doting lover.
"Oh Jerusalem, Jerusalem, how often have I longed to gather your children together, as a hen gathers her chicks under her wings, but you were not willing." (Luke 13: 34)

The Apostle John said it most clearly. *"Let us love one another because love is of God... Anyone who doesn't love, doesn't know God because God is love."*

iv) How to Live a Joyful, Meaningful Life

Jesus' teaching on this is best summarised in a poem called The Beatitudes, which means, 'how to be Happy or Blessed'.

The New Testament Greek word *makarioi* is often translated as "Blessed" or "Happy" but to our minds "blessed" doesn't really mean much and "happy" is too closely linked to pleasure. Jesus is referring to a deeper joy that comes from living a meaningful life. A joy that cannot be taken from us by circumstances.

The poem consists of eight pithy sayings describing eight attitudes of being that will lead to joy... eight be-attitudes.

Two versions of the poem can be found in the Gospels. There are differences between the versions but the overriding messages of the poems are the same.

> *Happy are the poor in spirit,*
> *for theirs is the Kingdom of Heaven.*
> *Happy are those who mourn,*
> *for they will be comforted.*
> *Happy are the meek,*
> *for they will inherit the Earth.*
> *Happy are those who hunger and thirst for righteousness,*
> *for they will be satisfied.*
> *Happy are the merciful,*
> *for they will be shown mercy.*
> *Happy are the pure in heart,*
> *for they will see God.*
> *Happy are the peacemakers,*
> *for they will be called the Sons of God.*
> *Happy are those who are persecuted because of righteousness,*
> *for theirs is the Kingdom of Heaven.*
>   (From Matthew's Gospel 5. 3 -10)

Unpacking the poem takes a bit of work and I think the guy who did the best job of it was Thomas Aquinas. Aquinas interprets the poem by breaking the eight sayings in two groups of four. Four negative beatitudes and four positives. The four negative beatitudes consider the four things that most people consider worthwhile; these are the goals of most lives. Jesus declares that all four of these things are dead ends in the quest for joy and meaning.

"*Blessed are the poor in Spirit*"
Don't seek **money**. Money will not satisfy your heart, it will not give you lasting joy.

"*Blessed are those who mourn*"
Don't seek **pleasure**. Pleasure doesn't last for long.

"*Blessed are the meek*"
Don't seek **power**. Power will not satisfy our hearts' desire.

"*Blessed are those who are persecuted*"
Do not seek popularity or **status**. Like all of the other negative beatitudes, status is transient.

None of the four possible objectives listed above can give us lasting joy or meaning. Yet these four are what drives most of human society. Most of us are constantly striving for money, power, pleasure or status, and none of us are happy.

Worse than just being dead ends, these four false goals have a dangerous addictive quality to them. When we seek to fill our lives or derive meaning through pursuing power or money or pleasure or status, we gain a brief rush but the feeling fades, leaving us yearning for more. We end up in a dangerous spiral of yearning, partial achievement, brief satisfaction, followed by an even greater yearning.

Don't misunderstand here. Jesus was not arguing that all pleasure, power, status or money are evil. It's a wonderful feeling to lie in a field and feel the sun warming your skin, or eating a well cooked meal, or being appreciated by others. These are all good things. But if we make our life's goal the pursuit of these four things, then we will become trapped in a cycle of misery and suffering not only for ourselves but for all of those around us.

Aquinas argues that most of the damage humans have done to the world and ourselves has been caused by making pleasure, power, wealth and status the central goals of our lives. So, what should be the central goals of our life if we want a meaningful, joyful existence? What are the four positive beatitudes?

"Happy are those who hunger and thirst for righteousness"
Strive for **goodness**. Being "good" or righteous should be as important to us as food or drink. Hunger for it. Thirst for it.

"Happy are the merciful"
Forgive the failings of others. Even those who are not sorry. Let love soak into your heart and pour out to everyone around you. Love your enemies because God is love.

"Happy are the pure in heart"
Keep your heat's desire primarily **focused** on being a child of God and loving as She does. There are many things that we desire and most of them are good and healthy. But to live a joyful and meaningful life, our primary focus must be on love, because God is love.

"Happy are the peacemakers"
If we are children of God, then we will do what God does. God's essential action is uniting, healing, reconciling. God wants to make peace because **God is love**.

These four attitudes mirror the attitudes of God as described by Jesus in the rest of the Gospels. If we try to be like God and commit ourselves to bringing about God's Kingdom of love and peace, then we will lead full, joyful lives.

That's your job, kids. Be the love of God in the world. That's what you were born to do. That's the only thing that will satisfy the yearning in your heart. Well, that's what Jesus believed, anyway.

Believing the Teaching of Jesus

Before we move on, let's just take a moment to think critically about the teachings of Jesus. I don't think anyone can argue that they are not beautiful, inspiring and uplifting. There's little wonder that many people who heard him were inspired to follow him, remember his message and then pass it on to others. But seriously, how can any rational person believe it?

In over twenty years of teaching, not one student ever said to me, "Seriously, Koch? That all sounds like bullshit to me." So, I've never discussed this in class, but for me, the hardest thing to believe by far is Jesus' claim that God loves us and we are Her children. It's a huge leap of faith! In my view the largest and most difficult leap in the entire journey.

We've established that if God exists, She must be eternal, transcendent and immanent, therefore the idea that this transcendent being loves us is good news indeed. But to then claim that we are children of this transcendent, eternal being, destined to grow up and become like Her... Well, that just seems crazy. We are, after all, just monkeys wearing shoes.

If God exists, She must eternally create and sustain the whole universe, but it doesn't necessarily follow that God must love everything She creates. When I'm painting a picture, I often create sections that are downright ugly, and I have to paint over them. When I'm building a garden bed, I do it for a function far beyond the pieces of wood or dirt that I use to create it. I may get some pride out of my creation but it's a very long bow to claim that I love the garden bed. A chicken lays an egg every day, but most times of the year, she leaves it in her nesting box and goes on with her life, completely indifferent to its fate. Why, other than human wishful thinking, should God be any different?

Here we come back to Aristotle. Our *pathos* might well lead us to want to believe the message of Jesus. If we want meaning in our lives, it's wonderful news to be told that the ultimate source of all meaning loves us. Any human yearning for meaning would want to believe it's true. But wanting something to be true, doesn't make it true.

On the other hand, we must be careful here, just because we want something to be true, doesn't mean it's *not* true. Our wishes and desires have zero weight on the reality of the universe.

Jesus was raised and taught firmly within the context of first century Judaism. The Jewish people had long believed that God loved them, so when Jesus taught about God's love, he was just "preaching to the choir." His Jewish audience would have been taught that from their earliest years and, like most of my students, it would have been inconceivable to imagine God existing and not loving them (his Greek or Roman audience, however would have found the teaching very radical. Greek and Roman deities were generally indifferent to humans). So, the idea that God loves us would dovetail neatly with Jesus' audience's *ethos*.

But Jesus' teaching about us being children of God would have been profoundly radical and flown hard in the face of his audience's *ethos*. It's one thing to believe that our creator loves us, but it is another thing entirely to claim that the creator is our father, and we are destined to grow up to become like this transcendent being. It's as if one of my gut fauna declared not just that I loved it, but that one day it would grow up to become like me. Sorry, little gut fauna, I really only think of you when you are making me sick and there is simply no way in the world that you are ever going to become a human being.

For people like me, who get caught up in their heads and love *logos*, the teaching of Jesus is sweet, poetic, even inspiring, but utterly ridiculous.

And yet, I believe it.

Sure, my family *ethos* and the Catholic culture in which I was raised make it easier for me than you. But there is another reason why I believe it, and I've already told you what it was.

I experienced the love of God in my room when I was 12 years old. For many, many people, throughout history, the teaching of Jesus did not merely stand on its own. Somehow, in ways we don't understand, the encounter with Jesus of Nazareth, either in person or via his stories and teaching, mediated an apophatic spiritual experience that validated his radical message.

In fact, there are many people who accept Jesus' teaching about the centrality love, without believing in him or even believing in the existence of God. This could be motivated by *pathos* or it could be *ethos* (probably a bit of both). But I think even those who have chosen to leap to the atheist bank of the creek, have still experienced the still small voice whispering in their hearts, telling them;

"Yes. This is true. You can trust love."

The Trial and Execution of Jesus

In other circumstances, Jesus would be remembered as a profound teacher within the Jewish religious tradition. He probably would have been quoted in the Talmud and remembered in the secular world in the same way as Rumi is remembered from the Islamic Tradition. But the controversy centering around the end of Jesus' life has forever catapulted him away from Judaism and into a contentious debate. Jesus would never be considered merely a wise teacher or a gentle poet. He would forever become a divisive figure. For either good or ill, the last days of Jesus' life were central to making him the most influential man who ever lived.

The basic facts of the controversy seem pretty clear. All four gospels agree that after Jesus challenged the authority of the Jewish religious leaders, he was arrested on a Thursday night and tried for blasphemy. The charge centred on the accusation that he had claimed to be the *Jewish Messiah*.

The legend of the Messiah was a long standing belief in first century Jewish religion. This legend had arisen over many years and contained several often vague and contradictory elements. By the time the Romans had established their rule in Palestine, this legend had become a powerful hope. In simplest terms, the Messiah was someone specially anointed by God to save the Jewish people from oppression, sin and death. For most first century Jews, this meant the physical overthrow of Roman imperial rule.

When Jesus was a boy, a man named Judas the Galilean had claimed to be the Messiah and led a revolt against Rome. His revolt was crushed and he and his followers were executed.

The Romans knew how dangerous this idea of a Messiah was and they made short work of anyone who claimed to be one.

One of the best known references to the Messiah in Jewish literature can be found in the book of Daniel:

> *"And I saw one like the son of man*
> *coming with the clouds of heaven.*
> *He was presented to the Ancient of Days.*
> *He was given authority, glory and sovereign power;*
> *all nations and peoples of every language worshiped him.*
> *His dominion is an everlasting dominion*
> *that will not pass away,*
> *and his kingdom is one that will never be destroyed."*
> Daniel Chapter 7.13-14

Notice the reference to people worshipping this "Son of Man". This would be deeply controversial to Jewish sensibilities. Jews believed in only one transcendent God and only God was worthy of worship. Any worship of something or someone other than God was Blasphemy.

Jesus never explicitly claimed to be the Messiah but according to Mark, the earliest of the gospels, he constantly called himself "the Son of Man". To contemporary ears, it sounds ambiguous, I mean we are all sons and daughters of 'Man'. But in first century Palestine, it was a direct reference to the quote from Daniel, and every Jewish listener knew what it meant. Jesus was claiming to be the Messiah.

This seems to contradict Jesus' general teaching that we are all Children of God and he was just one of many. Many scholars resolve this problem by suggesting that Jesus' understanding of himself as "Messiah" developed gradually over time. So there was his basic teaching, *"We are all children of God."* And then this slow realisation that occurred, later. *"I'm the Messiah, God's special agent sent to bring about the Reign of God."*

By the time of his trial this belief or realisation was fully developed. All four Gospels agree that he repeated the claim even more explicitly there.

> The high priest asked him, "Are you the Messiah? The son of the Blessed One?"
>
> "I am," said Jesus. "And you will see the Son of Man sitting at the right hand of the Mighty One and coming on the clouds of heaven." (Mk 14: 61-62)

Some people argue that the Jewish trial was a sham or in some way unfair, and it certainly can be argued that it would have been in the interests of The Gospel writers to make it seem so, but an honest reading of the sources, taking into account the historical context, makes it pretty clear that the trial was perfectly fair. After that outburst, the members of the Sanhedrin had a pretty simple choice: find Jesus guilty, or fall down and worship him.

For the Romans it was also a pretty open and shut case. Like all the phoney messiahs that had come before, Jesus was condemned to death by crucifixion the following morning.

Roman crucifixion is horrific. The victim is in constant agony and takes hours to die. All four sources agree that when faced with this, Jesus' closest followers fled, abandoning him to his fate. Once again, we can use the multiple sources test (all four gospels) and the test of embarrassment (the early church would be ashamed that none of their leaders stayed loyal to their founder).

Once the execution was completed, we have five sources that claim the body of Jesus was buried. The earliest reference is from Paul in a letter dated sometime in the fifties. The four Gospels add more detail, describing the burial as being carried out not by his disciples but by a member of the Jewish Sanhedrin, the Jewish Council that condemned him. Here too we have multiple sources and the embarrassment factor. The leaders of the Jesus movement were too scared to even try to bury his body. It was a sympathetic enemy who gave up his own tomb.

As the sabbath fell that Friday evening, the sad story seems to have come to its inevitable end. A good man, with a vision of humanity that was inspiring and optimistic, trying to make a difference under the heel of an oppressive regime, got swept up in his own importance and ended up alone and betrayed, dying in agony far from home.

Two thousand years later, we find ourselves staring at the embers of this extraordinary life and asking, *"What does this all mean?"*

8

Jesus: The Great Dilemma

The Disciples' Dilemma

Imagine it's the Friday night after Jesus was killed and we are sitting in the upper room with what is left of the disciples (The 'upper room' was the home base of Jesus and his disciples when he was in Jerusalem). You are sitting with Jesus' friends. How might they be feeling? What might they be talking about?

Of course, the dominant feeling would be grief. They loved their friend and mentor and his excruciating death would have been devastating for them. They would also be feeling shame, I suspect. Shame because they failed to stand beside him in his hour of need. But they may also be feeling shame for being taken in by a *false* Messiah.

It would be apparent to them that Jesus' claim to being the Messiah was false, because ultimately, he died. The legend of the Messiah was pretty clear. He was to save his people by bringing good news to the poor, proclaiming liberty to captives, giving sight to the blind and freeing the downtrodden from the oppressors' boot. He certainly wasn't meant to be arrested, beaten, tortured and die screaming in despair. What would they have made of it all?

Following G.K. Chesterton, it's reasonable to assume that the disciples were left in a very uncomfortable position. According to Chesterton, there were only three options:

1. Jesus claimed to be the Messiah when he knew he wasn't. Therefore, Jesus was a liar.
2. Jesus thought he was the Messiah when he wasn't. Therefore, Jesus was delusional.
3. Jesus was telling the truth. He really was the Messiah.

Jesus' execution would have ruled out any chance of the third option for the disciples in the upper room. Jesus died and the Kingdom was not established, leaving the disciples with only the first two options. Was he lying or was he deluded?

It's unlikely that Jesus would have lied, knowing what was in store for him. In fact, if he continued to lie even at his trial, it would make him seem more than just delusional. It would be crazy! That train of thought would likely rule out the first option.

The disciples would then be left with the tragic conclusion that Jesus was delusional. Despite his beautiful poetry and his sublime teaching, there would be no room for compromise in their minds.

In the present, we are in a similar situation. We're really stuck. He's either the Messiah or he's delusional. There is no middle ground. Let's explore these options.

Jesus' Dilemma

Why did Jesus think he was the Messiah? I have already hinted at the reason he may have thought this in the last chapter. His foundational spiritual experience on the banks of the river Jordan was as God's beloved Son.

Remember, spiritual experiences are apophatic. They cannot be explained in concrete language because language is based on finite, contingent reality and spiritual experiences take us into the realm of the transcendent. So, all spiritual experiences must be interpreted, not explained.

If we go back to our line of inquiry, Jesus seemed to interpret the message he received from God to be for everyone, not just for him. According to Jesus, we are all children of a loving God. So, if we are all the children of God, Jesus included, why then did he think he was special? Why did he think he was the Messiah?

There are two key sources for anyone's belief about their identity. Like us, Jesus would have internal spiritual experiences and external relational experiences. Both are important for helping us develop our identity.

Do you remember in a previous chapter I talked about my spiritual experience as twelve-year-old? Did that story prompt you to think about a spiritual experience you may have had? How did it make your feel? After my experience, I didn't want to share my story because I was ashamed. I didn't know if I believed it and above all I was worried people wouldn't believe me or if they did believe me, they would think I was crazy. I felt very uncertain.

I imagine Jesus would have felt similar after his spiritual experiences, like his experience at the river Jordan (from the previous chapter). He would have felt uncertain but he took a leap of faith. He *acted* on the insights he gained from his spiritual experience. He *acted* as if everyone he met was a child of God. He reached out and touched the sick, he forgave the sins of those assaulted by guilt, and challenged the authority of the religious and political leaders of his day.

There were also a number of external experiences which would have affected Jesus' sense of identity. All four gospels claim that miraculous healings took place when people encountered Jesus. It's very likely that these so called "miraculous healings" had a profound effect on Jesus' contemporaries. Could they also have been a reason why Jesus thought he was the Messiah? Let's look into these stories a little bit closer.

The Miraculous Healings Of Jesus

It's important to remind ourselves again, that the gospels are not history books. The purpose of the gospel writers was not to accurately describe everything that happened. They were trying to describe the apophatic spiritual encounters mediated through Jesus of Nazareth. The gospels are trying to explain the meaning of life using symbolic language, i.e., parables, stories, analogies and metaphor.

So when we look at the stories of the miracles of Jesus, we shouldn't try to analyse them as if they were articles in a contemporary newspaper. They are meant to be interpreted to explain the meaning and purpose of life and the nature of ultimate reality. So how can we use those gospels stories to work out why Jesus might have thought he was the Messiah?

Using our tests from earlier to assess the validity of the claims in the Bible (i.e., multiple sources, embarrassment, consistent voice, etc.) we don't have much to go on. The stories of the miraculous healings are often contradictory or at best hard to reconcile with each other. There are several stories of Jesus curing a blind person, but we don't know if these are multiple events or if they are different versions of the same symbolic story.

Another problem with the healing stories is that there was no contemporary medical science to test their condition. The story may say a man had leprosy, but what did that mean? Leprosy in first century Palestine ranged from a debilitating disease that rotted away a person's flesh, to eczema. When the gospels talk of Jesus casting out demons, we don't know if we are dealing with genuine demonic possession or if it was a form of mental illness, either mild or extreme.

There is always a temptation in these matters to leap to a narrow-minded view. Declare that because of the lack of consistency, the stories are all simply made up. They never happened and have nothing to tell us about the historical events. This would be a mistake.

Firstly, even today there are many stories of people recovering from illness in ways that can't be explained through modern medicine. We don't know everything about how the body works, and if you ask a doctor, they'd tell you that healing is as much art as it is science. So we can't rule out the possibility that encounters with Jesus actually caused people who were suffering from debilitating diseases to feel better.

Secondly, even though we don't know what the medical conditions of these people were before or after their encounters, as historians we are on pretty solid ground when we make this statement: many people who encountered Jesus of Nazareth claimed that he healed the sick.

In first century Jewish culture, people had a very different understanding of sickness to the understanding we have today. Sickness was seen as a sign of God's displeasure. There was suspicion and fear attached to the sick person and more often than not, they were ostracised from the community. Often it was considered tabu to even touch a person with a chronic illness. Imagine going through your life, deprived of human touch! Whatever health issue you had, it would certainly make it worse.

Therefore, if a person contracted chronic sickness, their family was often placed in a very difficult position. They had to either exclude the sick person or become excluded themselves. It would seem that different families reacted differently. The gospels tell stories of Jesus healing ostracised patients as well as those who were supported by their family members.

Jesus' Leap of Faith

How would Jesus have experienced the healings? Remember, Jesus believed that we were all children of God, made in the image and likeness of God and destined to share fully in the divine life. So how would he have reacted to the exclusion of those suffering from illness? The Gospels are very consistent here. It seems that Jesus refused to go along with the conventional wisdom. He accepted the sick and even reached out and touched them.

Jesuit Scripture scholar Jose Pagola, said Jesus, in keeping with his belief about the indwelling divinity of all humans, ignored the convention against touching and it may have been as much of a shock to him as it was to the patient, when the patient felt better.

Remember, Jesus had no medical training and probably shared the same medical understanding of his contemporaries. Imagine him reaching out in compassion to a sick, and lonely person and suddenly discovering that his touch healed the sick!

I am drawing a lot of long bows here, and we must be careful to recognise that this is mere conjecture. But if this were the case, it could explain why Jesus thought he was the Messiah. It certainly was part of the reason why his followers believed he was.

I'm going to talk about this more later on, but the spiritual is never certain. Our spiritual experiences are always subject to multiple possible interpretations. Our idea of God is constantly changing and developing, and our individual sense of purpose and identity is also never static and never certain. This is a characteristic that is inherent to all humans. Our finite minds are incapable of completely understanding transcendent reality, and Jesus was a human being with a finite mind.

Jesus' spiritual experience at the Jordan river, his experiences of healing the sick, his ongoing prayer and spiritual life had all contributed to his belief that God had called him and declared him to be the Messiah. This was a leap of faith, not an objective rational truth.

So when the high priest asked Jesus under oath to tell them if he was the Messiah, it must have gone straight to the heart of Jesus' sense of mission. Of course he wasn't sure he was the Messiah, but he had to make a call. He had to take a stand. He had to take a leap of faith. Was his vision true? This was not just about his own identity. The identity of everybody who had believed him when he told them they were children of God was at stake. Even if it meant his life, he couldn't deny his belief.

Did he hope that God would somehow save him? Maybe. Certainly there is some evidence from the early church that he did. But of course, there was no divine intervention. The heavens were silent as he died. Little wonder that three of the gospel writers state that from the cross came a cry of despair, "My God, my God, why have you abandoned me!"

The Greatest Cold Case of all Time

The resurrection of Jesus over 2000 years ago resolved the dilemma of Jesus' identity for the disciples. However, for us, the experience was not first hand and therefore still presents us with a dilemma. We have to grapple with a 2000-year-old cold case.

In detective work, cold cases are crimes in which the trail of evidence has run out and the perpetrator can no longer be found. Sometimes, an ambitious detective or family member may go back to the case and review the evidence in the hope of finding a clue or gaining an insight that had previously been missed. These cases are rarely solved but when they are, it's usually a cause for much excitement.

At the heart of the Christian story is a 2000-year-old cold case. What happened to the body of Jesus after he was crucified? Let's go back into the box of files and go through the evidence. Perhaps we might be able to find a clue that opens the case up again.

Our witnesses are five familiar sources. The four gospels and the letters of Paul of Tarsus. (The document Q, which we used earlier, seems to be silent on the final events of Jesus' life, focussing only on his teaching and sayings.) The five sources agree on some basic facts but disagree on others.

Firstly, all five claim that after his crucifixion, Jesus was buried. The gospels add that it was in a borrowed tomb and he was buried not by his disciples, but by a member of the Jewish Sanhedrin. The body that condemned him, and handed him over to the Romans for execution.

According to all four gospels, Jesus was taken down from the cross sometime late on Friday afternoon. The sun was setting, ushering in the sabbath and there was no time for the full burial rites. Joseph of Arimathea with the help of a few female disciples, placed the body in the tomb he had bought for his own use and a large stone was rolled over the entrance, sealing it shut.

Early on Sunday morning, once the sabbath (Saturday) was over, the female disciples returned to the tomb to complete the Jewish burial rituals. They claim to have found the stone rolled away and the tomb empty.

Now, if you went to visit the grave of a recently departed loved one and found it empty, what would you think? The first thing, I'd think is that I'd gone to the wrong grave. Once I'd ascertained that it was the right grave, I would certainly assume that someone or some thing (possibly a wild animal) had dug up my loved one's body. It would be a terrible realisation, and I would be deeply distressed.

The first disciples were no different. All four gospels describe a similar response. Except all the gospels include accounts of an extraordinary, spiritual encounters which convinced them that God had raised Jesus from the dead.

Remember, the gospel writers are not interested in writing history. They are trying to explain the meaning behind the apophatic spiritual experiences that gave their lives meaning. Therefore, the accounts have limited historical value to us. They are heavily laden with symbolic language and are often contradictory. But they all agree that many of Jesus' disciples had spiritual experiences that led them to believe that Jesus was "risen from the dead" (whatever that means. We will discuss that in more detail later).

What can we make of this cold case? It's never polite to simply discount a person's deeply held religious beliefs so we would have to tread gently about this claim of resurrection. Suffice it to say, that extraordinary claims require extraordinary evidence, and the claim that Jesus rose from the dead is about as extraordinary as you can get. So, who took the body? This is the great mystery; The cold case at the heart of 2000 years of history.

Let's line up the suspects. Who could have done this, who had motive and who had opportunity? These are the three questions we must wrestle with if we are to solve this mystery.

Suspect One: Some or All of the Disciples

The disciples were the ones blamed by the authorities from the very beginning of the controversy. Jewish and Roman leaders both said the disciples had stolen the body and spread the story of the resurrection.

Certainly, the women had the opportunity. They were the last to see the body and the first to see the tomb empty. But it's hard to believe they would have acted on their own. It is clear from the gospel accounts they were not believed by Peter or the other leaders of the disciples until they too had an apophatic spiritual encounter which convinced them.

Is it possible that all or at least a majority of the disciples were in on the crime? It was an unspeakably reprehensible crime in the Jewish tradition to desecrate any grave and if we were to accept them as the culprits, then we must argue they desecrated the grave of their beloved leader. Can you imagine digging up a loved one's grave to spread a lie? It's certainly not beyond the realm of possibility. But it would mean the first Christians had committed a crime that the vast majority of people (including them) would consider morally repugnant. How could they, in all conscience, have founded their movement if they knew the resurrection was a lie.

Again, this is not impossible, but if it were the case, we would expect to see signs of corruption, deceit and disrespect for humanity in other aspects of their lives. The historical record is quite clear here. The first Christians were accused of not having respect for traditional religions and being disturbers of the peace. But they treated each other and their enemies with kindness, and compassion.

What about their motive? According to political and religious authorities of the day claiming Jesus had risen created quite a stir. But why would the disciples want to do this? In today's world, it may be reasonable to think they would be tempted by the promise of founding their own religion, with all the power and wealth that comes with it. But in the Roman Empire founding a new religion in opposition to the state sanctioned ones, was not the path to a successful life.

Because of their beliefs, the first Christians were poor and ostracised. Many of them died excruciating, violent deaths because of their claim that God had raised Jesus from the dead.

Even under torture, we have no record of any Christian admitting to Roman authorities that they had made up their story or stole the body. If any of the disciples had done this, we can be sure that the authorities would have publicised it and made that person's name known.

Finally, we have the problem of the sudden, radical change in behaviour of the disciples between the trial of Jesus and their post Easter relationship with the Roman authorities. When the temple police arrived with clubs to arrest Jesus in the garden of Gethsemane, the disciples fled. Most of them scattered and hid, not even being present at the trial or execution. After their Easter experiences, the disciples faced the authorities fearlessly. Proclaiming their message of a messiah who had conquered death in spite of threats of death, torture and crucifixion. What caused the change?

The only reasonable explanation for this sudden lack of fear is that the first disciples genuinely believed that Jesus had risen

from the dead. They no longer feared those who could kill them. In one of their early songs, they would sing:
Oh death where is thy victory?
Oh death where is thy sting?

The Other Suspects

Could the Roman Authorities have taken Jesus' body? Of all the possible suspects, the Religious and political leaders had the best motive. It would not have been in their interests for a tomb of this dead Messiah to become a rallying point for his followers. It would make perfect sense for the Roman Governor (Pontius Pilate) to change his mind about allowing Jesus to be buried and merely remove the body and dispose of it.

Unlike the Jewish disciples of Jesus, they had no moral qualms about disposing of bodies. They disposed of most crucified bodies. The Romans weren't bound to keep the sabbath holy. There would have been nothing to stop them from taking the body on Saturday. They had motive and they had opportunity.

If the authorities had done this, however, all that was required to crush the story of the resurrection, was for the Romans to declare that they had removed the body and disposed of it. But they did not. They stuck to their story, blaming the disciples. And the story grew.

It is possible that someone, who was not constrained by Jewish religious sensibilities stole the body and hid it, just for shits and giggles. That would be a pretty funny thing. Imagine some wack job steals the body and the next thing he knows, a whole new religion springs up and people are getting killed. Of course, it would be very unlikely that someone would do such a thing and not tell another soul. Eventually some story would come out and the authorities would have leapt at it.

Could Jesus' body have been *'taken'* by The Lord, the God of Israel? The first problem with this, of course, is that we don't know whether God exists or not. So it's hard to claim Her as a suspect. But if we have taken a leap of faith and believed that God exists, then She has both motive and opportunity.

In the Jewish religious tradition, God was all powerful so God was able to raise the dead. In terms of motive, the first Christians were convinced that by raising Jesus from the dead, God had utterly vindicated his teaching and his claims. It was as if God overturned the legal ruling of the Jewish Sanhedrin and the Roman execution. Jesus was the Messiah and everything he said about himself and about us was true.

In the first century, when the case was fresh, only two of these options were taken seriously. All the historical evidence from the first century proposed that public opinion was sharply divided into two camps. Those who claimed that the disciples stole the body and those who claimed that God raised Jesus from the dead.

In the next section, I am going to talk about some more recent attempts to solve the mystery.

Our Dilemma: The Physical Resurrection of Jesus

I have to tell you up front here, kids. I believe in the resurrection. It's an idea that I have given my heart to. I have taken the leap of faith. There are many people who have given their heart to the idea of the resurrection and not all of them actually believe that Jesus of Nazareth rose from the dead on the first Easter Sunday nearly 2000 years ago. Some of them wouldn't even identify as Christians, but they have still given their heart to the idea of resurrection. I will discuss this in more detail later on, but for now, I want to focus on a more concrete interpretation.

When I say I believe in the resurrection, I also believe that on that first Easter Sunday, the tomb was physically empty because God raised Jesus from the dead. The Roman and Jewish Authorities could not find the body and could not find the one who stole it, because it wasn't stolen, it was resurrected.

I will discuss what I mean by resurrected later, but for now I want to discuss the reasons why I believe this to be the case. Firstly, of course, my family *ethos* was strongly in favour of believing it. My parents believed it, most of my teachers believed it. When I was a child, my brother and sister believed it. Whilst I knew there were many who did not, it didn't feel as outrageous to me as it probably does to you.

Secondly, my *pathos* is strongly in favour of believing in the resurrection. There is something terribly tragic about this innocent man, who proclaimed such a wise and wonderful message. Who was led by his inner spirituality to believe that we were all children of God and that God loves us, who was betrayed, abandoned, tortured and executed without his loving

God lifting a (metaphorical) finger to help him. I really want Jesus to have been resurrected. I really want him to be the Messiah, and I really want what he said about God, life and our ultimate meaning and purpose to be true. As I've said elsewhere, if Jesus wasn't the Messiah, he *ought* to have been. If love is not our origin and ultimate end, it *ought* to be. If God exists, *She ought to be like Jesus.*

But aside from those motivations, my *logos* actually believes, despite the ludicrous claim, that it actually happened. Of course, I am not at all certain of this but if I am pressed, I will say that even though I don't know what happened to the body of Jesus, on balance of probabilities, I believe the disciples' story. I believe he was raised from the dead.

In the previous section, I discussed the various suspects that were considered by those contemporary to the events. In the first century, there were only two main theses. The first, proposed by the political and religious authorities, was that the body was stolen by Jesus' disciples. The second was proposed by the disciples. They argued that God had raised Jesus from the dead. For those closest to the controversy, they were the only legitimate arguments.

Given what we now know about history and human behaviour the claim that the disciples stole the body seems more implausible than it was when Ciaphas and Pilate first proposed their explanation. But the alternative, that God raised Jesus from the dead, is still just as unbelievable now as it was then. Since those days, several attempts have been made to explain the disappearance of Jesus' body, and refute the claims of the resurrection. I don't find any of them compelling.

One of the theories is the swoon theory. According to this argument, Jesus didn't die on the cross, only fainted or swooned. The Romans then took down his unconscious body and Joseph of Arimathea buried him, without noticing that he was still alive. Then in the cool of the tomb, Jesus woke up and walked away. This theory helps explain the appearances to the disciples because they could then have seen the wounded Jesus and exaggerated the story into a resurrection.

The strength of the argument is that it explains almost all of the facts of the case and doesn't require any sort of transcendent intervention. Its great weakness is in its implausibility.

When the swoon theory was first proposed in the 1800's, they didn't know as much about crucifixion as we do today. Roman crucifixion was brutally simple. Once the victim collapsed due to exhaustion, they were unable to get air into their lungs and died from asphyxiation. Had Jesus swooned, he would have died within minutes. This explains why in all the centuries of Roman civilisation, there has not been one single case of a botched crucifixion. Not even a hint or a legend of a person surviving.

In addition to this problem, the theory would have us believe that Jesus recovered in the tomb without any food, water or medical aid, rolled away the stone with bleeding hands and walked away on shattered feet.

Of course, the theory is not completely impossible, but if I was writing a novel, I wouldn't use this as a plot device.

A second theory is that Jesus' body wasn't buried. This theory argues that the rules of multiple attestation (i.e., the multiple written stories) and embarrassment (i.e., if the story is embarrassing it is more likely to be true) are suspended after Jesus dies on the cross. From then on, the whole story becomes metaphor. One of the main advocates of this theory is a man named John Dominic Crossan (1934-), an excellent theologian who believes in Jesus and has given his heart to the idea of the resurrection (I'll say more on this later).

Crossan argues that after execution, the Romans did not allow their victims to be buried. Their bodies were either left to rot on the cross or they were thrown into a mass grave. Therefore, there was no burial and no empty tomb. The visions of the disciples were purely spiritual experiences and there was no physical aspect to the resurrection.

It's a short step, for those who don't believe in the resurrection to then say that the spiritual experiences of the disciples were just wishful thinking or grief inspired hallucinations.

Once more, this argument has reasonable breadth because it accounts for nearly all of the facts but there is one fatal problems with it. Archeology has shown the premise of the entire argument to be false.

The basic premise is that victims of crucifixion were never buried, therefore Jesus was not buried. But in 1968 the bones of a crucified man were excavated in a tomb in Jerusalem. The bones were found in an ossuary or bone box and inscribed on the box was the man's name, 'Yehohanan son of Hagakol'. The bones were dated to before the destruction of Jerusalem in 70 AD so very close in time to the death of Jesus. This man was clearly crucified (one of the nails was still embedded in his foot) and he was buried. All his bones were present and the ossuary was placed in the family tomb.

The discovery is fascinating for many reasons but for our purposes, it drives a silver spike through the heart of the no tomb argument. The statement, "victims of Roman crucifixion weren't buried" is conclusively shown to be false.

Of course this doesn't mean that all the victims of crucifixion were buried but it means that you cannot use this as a premise for an argument. It is an archeological certainty that *some* crucifixion victims in first century Palestine were buried and every contemporary literary source claims that Jesus of Nazareth was one of them. There was not a single Roman or Jewish source from the first few centuries that challenged the claim that Jesus was buried.

There are five separate literary sources claiming it and the fact that he was buried by a member of the Jewish ruling class and not his disciples was a source of embarrassment to the early church. If it weren't for the mystery surrounding disappearance of his body, there would be nothing remotely controversial about the burial of Jesus.

Philosophical Objections

Before I move on, I should address the philosophical objections to the question of the resurrection because despite the fact that most of the arguments have focussed on the physical and historical issues, the main opposition to the idea of the resurrection stems from a philosophical position, that is often unstated and therefore, untested.

The first and most obvious philosophical argument is that God couldn't have raised Jesus from the dead because God doesn't exist. This argument sits behind many of the objections. But strictly speaking it's not an argument. Of course, if God doesn't exist, She couldn't have raised Jesus from the dead, but these two negatives, set out in this premise and conclusion format, tell us exactly nothing. If Napoleon didn't exist, he couldn't have invaded Russia. That statement is true, but it tells us nothing about whether Napoleon invaded Russia or not. This argument against the resurrection is simply a statement of faith.

"I believe there is no God so Jesus wasn't raised from the dead."

"Good for you... my favourite colour is blue."

A more substantial argument (and personally the one I find most convincing) is that God doesn't act that way. There is no evidence that God directly intervenes in human history or suspends the laws of nature in this way. No-one has ever been raised from the dead before or since. When a person dies, they stay dead, and God doesn't stop the game and put the chess piece back on the board.

At one level, this argument is irrefutable. Despite all our prayers, and all the countless good and holy people who have died, no one has been raised from the dead. If God exists, then it seems like raising the dead is not one of the things She does.

But Christians claim that the resurrection of Jesus is a unique event. It is not something that happens sometimes, or even rarely. It is a once-off phenomenon that occurred at the centre of history. (I'll talk more about that later on.) It's not reasonable to argue that a one off event cannot occur because it's never happened before or since.

Take for example the Big Bang, that cosmologists believe began the universe. It is a unique event. We can't argue against the Big Bang by saying that there has never been (to our knowledge) another Big Bang, before or since. It is true that we know of no other Big Bangs, but that in no way refutes the existence of the Big Bang. It's unique... a one off event that (probably) won't happen again. In the same way the resurrection of Jesus was unique.... A one off event that (probably) has never happened before and (probably) will never happen again.

So we find ourselves in another difficult position with regards to the Great Dilemma. Was Jesus the Messiah with a definitive insight into the meaning of life or was he good man who was tragically deluded. Was the life and teachings of Jesus uniquely validated by God through the resurrection or did his body disappear through human agency? All the proposed explanations for the empty tomb are quite implausible.

The most intellectually honest response to the question of the resurrection is therefore, that we simply don't know. Jesus remains a disturbing figure, shrouded in mystery. We are not free to dismiss him with false certainty. He stands alone amongst the great pageant of human kind, beyond our understanding or our pity.

Who is the third who walks always beside you?
When I count, there are only you and I together
but when I look ahead up the white road
there is always another one walking beside you
gliding wrapt in a brown mantle, hooded
I do not know whether a man or a woman
— but who is that on the other side of you?

T.S. Elliot (from The Wasteland)

9

Giving your Heart to Jesus

Another Leap of Faith

In the last chapter we pondered whether Jesus was a brilliant but fundamentally deluded preacher or whether he had a unique insight into the meaning of life. Did God really raise Jesus from the dead thus vindicating everything he said and did? Or, did the disciples steal his body and establish the church on a lie? We simply don't know.

When it comes to Jesus' life and resurrection, *logos* has taken us as far as it can on our journey. We have come to another creek that crosses our path. Another leap of faith beckons. But this is a different kind of leap to the previous one.

When confronting the question of the existence of God, we had no choice. We had to leap, either to belief or unbelief, because without making that leap, our quest for meaning would fail. In this instance, at this new creek, we don't need to decide whether we believe in Jesus or not. There's nothing to compel us to decide for or against Jesus, his message and his resurrection. We can declare that we just don't know and look elsewhere for insights into the nature of God and the quest for meaning.

In Chapter three, I told you that an opinion is a statement we think is true based on our reason but to believe is to give your heart to something. This is what we need to find meaning in life. We need a particular type of leap of faith. We need to give of our heart to something. No opinion can give our lives meaning.

There are many people who *think* Jesus rose from the dead but they have not given their heart to the idea because they don't live as if it's true or if it matters. There are many people who *think* Jesus was the Son of God but they live as if their lives are only encompassed within the material world and the endless pursuit of money, status, pleasure and popularity. They might *say* they believe in Jesus but their actions in life do not embody his purpose and mission. They may *think* Jesus was the son of God, but they have not really given their hearts to the idea. Their lives are still meaningless.

When I tell you that I believe in Jesus, what I mean is that I have given my heart to him. I accept that what Jesus said was true and have thrown my lot in with him. It means I try to act as if we are all children of God and destined to share fully in the divine life, even though I often find this a difficult opinion to hold.

When I say I believe in the resurrection of Jesus, I mean that I have given my heart to the idea that good will triumph over evil and love will triumph over death. I cling to this in my heart. It informs and empowers my life even though I often find the sheer bloody minded optimism of it too much to handle.

So, we find ourselves at the creek, facing a great leap of faith that can give our lives meaning. What we think about history or philosophy cannot give our lives meaning. Only an open-hearted leap of faith can can do this. There are other religious traditions that also provide meaning to people's lives, but they too require a similar, open-hearted leap of faith.

Because of this, as we prepare ourselves to make this great leap of faith and try to trust in the message and person of Jesus, we look up and see some of our atheist brothers and sisters waiting for us on the far side of the creek.

Remember, they took the leap to declare that there was no God and life had no meaning. They were forced to make up their own meaning. To find meaning, they took a different leap of faith. They create meaning by living as if we all have an inherent dignity and that love and goodness is greater that hate and death. They give their heart to that idea and derive meaning by living as if it were true. And why not? It's as good a meaning system as any. Many of us end up at the same bank of the creek, but have very different journeys to get there.

When the first disciples experienced Jesus risen from the dead, they too gave their hearts to this great idea, and just as we found when we leapt across the first creek, they found reason waiting for them on the other side. For now, come with me. Make a tentative leap across the creek and believe that Jesus existed, died and was resurrected. Remember, you can always jump back again later.

What are we giving our heart to?

The resurrection can be seen as God's complete vindication of everything Jesus said and did. Those who believe in the resurrection see Jesus as uniquely representative of who God is and what the meaning of life is.

Remember God, who is the source of all meaning, is immanent in the universe, but She's hidden behind finite reality. It's as if this infinite meaning, that is always present, erupted into full view in the life, death and resurrection of Jesus of Nazareth. It's as if God has placed this one great anecdote right in the middle of the story of humanity to provide the perfect lens through which everything else can be understood.

The first disciples, and many Christians (including me) believe that this great story is historically true. But more than that, all Christians believe that the story is *more* than just historically true. We believe that embedded within that story is the supreme revelation of the nature of ultimate reality and the meaning of life.

In this sense, whether you believe in its historical reality or not, the life, death and resurrection of Jesus becomes more than a story. It becomes *myth*.

In today's rationalist culture, myths are often defined as stories that aren't true. But that is not the original definition of myth and it does not account for why humans create them, share them, and have handed them on for centuries.

Myths, like metaphor, analogy, symbol and ritual, are another form of symbolic language. They are not simply "true" or "not true". Myths are stories that are beyond the simple categories of "true" or "false". A myth is a story that attempts to shed light on the ultimate nature of reality, and the meaning of life. Each myth is a spotlight, shining on the statue of transcendent meaning. That's why some theologians describe myths as being "more than true."

There is no point asking if the events depicted in a myth actually occurred. That is not the purpose of myth. "The Ugly Duckling" is more than a story. It is a myth. It tries to tell us something about growth, acceptance and true beauty. The story is not about ducks, it's about us and how we view ourselves and others. The Ugly Duckling is more than true.

The story of the life, death and resurrection of Jesus is also more than true. It is a myth. Christians believe that it's the great myth in which all of our hearts' desires are fulfilled. That's a pretty heavy burden to put on one story but that's what Christians believe. We call this myth *the Paschal Mystery*.

In theological language, a *mystery* is not simply something that we do not or cannot understand. A mystery in theological language is *an infinitely knowable reality*. We can think about it over and over, coming to new and fruitful insights, and never exhaust the meaning or lessons we can learn from it. Mysteries and myths have a lot in common but a myth is a type of story and a mystery is more of a concept, an idea or a doctrine. The Paschal Mystery is a combination of both.

There are other mysteries in Christian theology (I'll talk to you about another big one later), but every great insight of Christianity, every mystery, is actually embedded in and dependent on the myth called the Paschal Mystery. You don't have to be a Christian to give your heart to the Paschal Mystery and as I've said earlier, plenty of Christians haven't genuinely given their hearts to it. But when you do, your life is never the same. Those who have given their hearts to it do not escape suffering, failure, and death, but these things fit into a bigger system of meaning.

The Paschal Mystery

Like any symbolic story, the Paschal Mystery must be interpreted, not explained. I find the best way to interpret the Paschal Mystery is by looking at it from different angles and at different levels. I'm just going to run through two interpretations here, but there are many more.

Firstly, the rich, the powerful or the popular are not always right. For example, Jesus was seen as a pauper, an insurrectionist and a criminal. He was condemned by the religious and political authorities of the day. The most powerful and important, the wisest and most respected people in the system of the time, combined to condemn this man, exclude him from their community and inflict a horrific death on him. But God waves away human power, authority, wealth and status in a blink of an eye, turning everything on its head. The condemned outcast suddenly is resurrected and exalted, raised to share the very throne of God Herself (Remember the prophecy of the Messiah from Daniel). Reality is not how the world system sees it.

As the prophet Isaiah wrote:

For my thoughts are not your thoughts,
Nor are your ways my ways, says the Lord.
For as the heavens are higher than the Earth,
So are my ways higher than your ways
And my thoughts higher than your thoughts. (Is: 59:9)

Jesus then becomes a metaphor for all those condemned and rejected.

Not everyone who is condemned or cast out is innocent and most of them are not killed. But also, it's not just the powerful who exclude and condemn. We exclude people all the time on the basis of money, power, education, appearance, health or personality. Jesus is a metaphor for all of these people. Anyone who we consider unacceptable takes the role of Jesus in this metaphor.

Because of God's vindication in the resurrection, Jesus becomes a metaphor for God Herself. When we condemn, ostracise and punish, we are condemning God. Because everyone is a son or daughter of God and has the dignity that stems from that identity.

If we truly give our hearts to Jesus and the Paschal Mystery, then there are no "goodies" and "baddies," no in-group or out-group. No one is acceptable or unacceptable. We are all children of one loving God. We are all both victims and victimisers.

A second interpretation is the notion that everyone who has ever lived will be (and in some sense already is) raised to live forever in God. Jesus suffered terribly with no way of understanding whether his suffering had any purpose. This lack of understandable purpose is a crucial element in all human suffering.

From the cross, Jesus cried out, "My God, my God, why have you abandoned me?" This is a common experience of all of us when we suffer. We feel as if God has abandoned us. I have felt this many times in my life and I'll probably experience it many times more. So will you.

Jesus' abandonment by God was never resolved. He died alone in agony with no idea of his suffering's purpose. But God raised him up on the third day and exalted him into a new and glorious life.

Swiss theologian, Karl Barth says, there was no greater divine moment in the life of Jesus than when he cried out "My God! My God! Why have you abandoned me?" In other words, this was God Herself suffering on the cross. Barth then says that Jesus was never more human than when he was resurrected. Because he did not raise himself, he was raised!

This pattern of death and resurrection seems to be deeply embedded in reality. According to contemporary scientific cosmology, long before our sun existed, primordial stars exploded, scattering their heavy elements across the galaxy. These heavy elements, carbon, oxygen, nitrogen and others, found their way into a new gas cloud that became our solar system.

Look at your hand. All the atoms that make up your hand were formed in the heart of a star. All the basic building blocks of your entire body were born in a star. You are star dust. But that star had to die, so that you and all life could live. Death and resurrection.

Those same atoms that are now part of your body have been recycled through tectonic activity and living processes for the entire history of Earth. You do not own those atoms. They are just yours for now. Some of them may have been part of an early volcano, some of them may have been part of an ancient dinosaur, and some of them may have been part of another human who lived, loved and 'wept when it was all done, for being done too soon'. Your very existence is dependent on the death of all those. And one day, you will surrender your atoms back to the great cycle of death and resurrection.

The myth of death and resurrection is embedded in various forms through nearly every human culture and religious tradition. But in the Paschal Mystery, this reality is taken even further. Jesus didn't simply die and have his body used as raw material for another life form. God raised him from the dead in a new 'body'. God rescued Jesus from the cycle. This resurrected Jesus never dies. His essence remains forever in God. This is an ultimate resurrection.

This resurrection is not exclusive to Jesus. According to the paschal mystery, this is the ultimate destiny of all life. Everyone who has ever lived will be raised to live forever in God.

It sounds ludicrous, I know. Even as I'm writing this, I'm squirming a bit, because my rational mind is shaking its head in disbelief. But this is what the myth says. I am torn between my instinctive disbelief and my own profound yearning...

Oh please, God... let it be true.

The Paschal Mystery in my Life

The Paschal Mystery does not just describe the pattern of death and resurrection in nature. It is also a powerful metaphor for our daily lives. In two months I'll turn 64 years old and as I look back on more than half a century of memory, I can see an unmistakable pattern of death and resurrection.

Moving house and leaving my friends in primary school was a cause of genuine grief for me. I mourned them, I thought about them and imagined that there would be some way to reconnect. But of course, time passed, I made new friends and found a new life in my new town.

Leaving primary school and going to high school was also quite traumatic for me, as I had to let go of my primary school reality and head into the painful, difficult world of adolescence. Being dumped by my girlfriend, losing table tennis grand finals, losing friends, losing jobs and election defeats – all of these were little deaths and each of them brought their own suffering. But each was also a necessary prelude to a new life. Each little death gave way to a little resurrection.

I remember the day after my daughter Emily died, I sat on the toilet and tried to work out how much longer I would have to live. I was about 48 years old and I remember thinking that I've probably got at least another thirty years to go. Thirty long years of emptiness and sorrow. I used to say in those days, "I really liked the person that I used to be. That Darren Koch fella was a nice guy. But he's gone now and he's not coming back."

But gradually, almost imperceptibly, small, green shoots appeared and a new life began. I was right, the old Darren Koch died in April 2009 but a new Darren arose. In many ways the new Darren was completely different to the old Darren, but of course it was still me. The old Darren remains embedded in the resurrected Darren.

It took me a long time to realise this pattern in my life. I had heard it many times as I was growing up, but it took decades for me to grasp it in my heart and soul. To actually believe in it and trust it. In 2019, I crashed out of teaching. My capacity to function in a classroom just collapsed. I was angry and frustrated, and simply unable to do the job anymore. The collapse came surprisingly quickly and I went from being a popular, extremely competent, well-respected educator to a laughing stock, barely able to function within the constraints of the law.

But by that stage, I had learned to trust the great promise of the Paschal Mystery. Every death leads to a resurrection. And sure enough, a new Darren rose out of the ashes of the old.

There will be other deaths for me, and I'm sure they will be painful, but I believe there will be resurrections too. The last thing you will know about me will be a death. By the time you read this, you'll probably know how I died. Whether it was quick or slow. Did I go out peacefully, with dignity, or was it a brutal, excruciating dismantling that left me broken not just physically but psychologically and spiritually as well?

Whatever it will be, I hope that death will not have the last word. God will have the last word. And God's word is love, forgiveness and resurrection. I don't know if God will raise me from my final death, but I'm going to act as if She is going to, because that's what God has always done. After each little death, there was a resurrection, so why shouldn't there be a final resurrection after my final death?

Giving your Heart in the Face of Death

I have a feeling that you will not read this book until you are facing death. Either the possibility of your own death or the death of someone you love. The old saying goes: There is nothing like death to make us think about life. Death brings the terrible meaninglessness of life to the front of our consciousness and demands that we face it head on. It challenges whatever worldview we may have adopted and asks, "Do you really believe this?"

After the death of his wife, C.S. Lewis described this experience as if he were standing at the top of a cliff with a thick rope coiled on the ground at his feet. If someone were to ask him, "Can that rope hold your weight over this cliff?" He would say, "Yes." But if he were then tied to that rope and lowered off the edge of the cliff, then all his certainties would disappear very quickly.

That's how it is when we face death. When we're young and life seems to stretch on indefinitely, we can think whatever we like, and assume that our belief system will "hold our weight". But when we are caught in the terrifying gaze of Death, then all our doubts arise.

That certainly happened to me. Before Emily died, I believed in the story of Catholic Christianity. I believed in resurrection and the ultimate triumph of Love over Death. But after she died, everything came crashing down. I was lost and couldn't explain my situation to anyone.

I remember telling my sister, Valerie, "It's as if I've been told a terrible secret that nobody wants to know." She didn't reply. She didn't ask what the secret was and I couldn't have told her, even if I wanted to. At the time, I would have said something like, "We're all going to die... everyone... everyone I love, everyone I've ever known... and me too... we're going to die. And there's nothing we can do about it."

But that wasn't the secret. Of course we're all going to die. Every adult knows that but after Em died, it wasn't just something I knew intellectually, it was something I felt deeply in my bones. It cast its shadow over my waking hours and haunted me at night in my dreams. Terrible dreams of death, grief and horror. Nothing was safe, even sexual dreams turned into nightmares where my lover would turn into a rotting corpse.

I was haunted, and I was angry at everyone else because they were not, and I couldn't share my horror with them because I didn't want them to end up cursed like me. I loved them too much to impose that on them, but I resented them for their innocence.

People who sprouted comforting religious platitudes made we want to scream.

"I feel her close to me."
I don't. She's dead.
"She's in a better place."
How do you know that!?
"Her suffering is over."
Is it? Is it really?
"There's a new angel in heaven now."
Oh, fuck off!
"She'll live forever in our memories."
That is pure, unadulterated horseshit!

When talking about death, why do people sprout shit that's clearly not true? Nobody lives forever in our memories. That's one of most painful things about death.

Within days of Emily's death, my memories of her started to fade. At first, I forgot the minutiae of daily events from years past. Then I realised I was forgetting more recent things. As time went on, I began to forget the shape of her hands, the curve of her back and the size of her ears. Then her mannerisms began to disappear into caricature, until now all I have are a few shattered fragments. The sound of her laugh, her giving a speech in a debate, her in Fiji hitching up her skirt after mass so she can ride a horse. She dies again every day as another memory disappears... each little death is another excruciating loss.

But that was still not the great secret. I didn't realise what the secret was until a few years later. I was cooking porridge in my little flat in Frankston and complaining to God about death and its horror and its inevitability. When suddenly, like a flash I realised, that I didn't believe. In my heart of hearts I didn't believe that she had "gone to heaven" or "was held safely in God." I just didn't believe it. In my deepest heart, I believed she was dead, it was over, there was no coming back and no God to raise us from the dead. It was all just sad, wishful thinking.

I remember staring at the pot of half cooked porridge, gripping the wooden spoon so tightly that I thought it might break. I knew enough Catholic theology to know that faith was a gift given by God. And it was by Grace we were saved. It was nothing we earned. I remember staring up at the ceiling, the metaphorical abode of God, and raging.

"Fuck you! You let my daughter die, left me broken and then don't even give me the gift of faith! Bullshit! Not happening! You can keep your pathetic little gift of faith. I'm bloody stealing it! I'm going to believe in the Christian story in a stubborn act of sheer will and you can take your gift of faith and shove it up your arse!"

Even as I said it, I knew. I felt in my heart that familiar burning. Something else was going on that I didn't understand. I still don't fully understand but I think I realise now that we are not saved by what we think. We are saved by what we choose to give our hearts to. It's the will to act as if the Paschal Mystery is true, even if you *think* that it's not.

The Leap of Faith: Jumping off The Table

One of my earliest memories is when I was about two or three years old. My dad would stand my older brother and sister on the kitchen table and they would jump from the table into his arms. He would swing them around and land them safely on the floor. Then they would climb up on the table and leap again, squealing in delight.

I remember him putting me on the table and holding out his arms, "Jump, Darren," he said with an inviting smile.

I stood there staring at him. Refusing to jump.

"Come on, Son. Don't be afraid. I won't drop you."

I vividly remember staring at his face, his arms, the floor (so far away) and thinking, you don't want to drop me, but you can't be sure that you won't.

I never jumped off that table. I still remember his face (so young and innocent) and the hurt and disappointment on it. But I never jumped. I just wasn't much of a believer.

But now, over sixty years later, I jump. I jump all the time. Never knowing whether She'll catch me or not. Expecting to be dropped but acting as if She won't. Usually I'm caught, and I'm pleasantly surprised but even when I am dropped and I hit the floor, I get up, climb back on the table and jump again. Because that's the only way to live a full life.

I could choose to live my life as if I was never going to fall, but that would be a denial of reality. I could choose to not think about falling, but that requires more will than I have and it seems to me a kind of flat, unreflective, life. I could choose to believe that I will eventually fall and never get up, that death will have the last word. But having buried my daughter, my parents, and other people who I have really loved, I don't want to live in a world where death has the last word. I don't think I could.

So, I take my leap of faith. I give my heart to Jesus, his message and the Paschal Mystery. I live as if God has the last word. Maybe She does and maybe She doesn't. There's nothing inherently irrational about either position. One alternative seems good for me and another seems bad. But why should the good alternative be any less realistic than the bad? As an interpretive lens for my life, the Paschal Mystery works, as it has worked for countless people before.

10

Who is Jesus?

Who am I? Who are you?

In the last chapter, we decided to take a tentative leap of faith to "believe" that Jesus of Nazareth was raised from the dead and the Paschal Mystery was the primary metaphor for meaning in life. We then looked at some of the the logical implications of that position and what that meant for our quest for meaning. In this chapter, we're going to look at more implications of the Paschal Mystery in the hope of unveiling more about the meaning of our lives. Remember, this chapter assumes a *tentative* decision in favour of the resurrection. You don't need to have made a commitment or total leap of faith, we are simply assuming that Jesus was raised from the dead so as to explore the possible implications.

It was early December. The senior students had finished their exams and left school. The juniors were winding down towards holidays, so we took a group of year nines to the Holocaust museum as part of their History and RE curriculum.

We wandered through exhibits with familiar photographs of emaciated victims and obscure memorabilia of the Nazi horror. At the end of the tour, we were ushered into a lecture theatre where a small elderly woman told us her story.

She had been a child who had survived Auschwitz, but her parents, siblings and her entire extended family died there. Because she had given this talk so many times before, she told her story with a casual air. She felt no need to emphasise the horror or even discuss the emotions. She mentioned her emotional scarring only in passing, saying she still gets nightmares sometimes.

As the supervising teacher, I went up to thank her at the end of her talk. She smiled at me and as I looked into her eyes, I found myself swept up in a grief I couldn't explain. I started crying. Softly at first, but then when she reached out her hand to touch my shoulder I erupted into sobs. The lecture hall went silent as I fought for control.

"I'm sorry," I gasped.

She looked at me in a mixture of concern and wonder, "Who are you?" she asked.

"I'm nobody," I replied between sobs.

"Oh..." she said "I thought, maybe ..." and then her words trailed away.

"I'm just really sorry that this happened to you," I said lamely.

She wanted to know why I was so upset. When she asked me who I was, she wasn't asking my name or where I was born or my job. She saw me reacting in a way that was different from others. She thought because of my reaction that I might have a connection to her story that others did not. I could not have answered her question by telling her my name, my race or even my entire life story. My reaction was coming from a place deeper than all of those things. Her question was targeting my *identity*: the essence of who I was. In effect she was asking, "Who are you, that you feel so deeply about this matter?"

This question of a person's identity it not simple. I know there is a person I describe as "me ". But the essence of that person is fundamentally mysterious. There is more to who me are than my name, my age, my family and my life story. There is something deep within me, my essence that makes me, me.

When you were a baby having your nappy changed or a child playing in a sand pit, or a teenager reading a book, you were still the same person. You may feel different. You may think differently. You may have have had different experiences, but your identity remained the same. You were still you.

Your body doesn't make you, you. The cells of our body are constantly dying and being replaced. The body you have now is almost completely different to one you had ten years ago, and in ten years time, it will be completely different again.

You don't create your own identity by your thoughts, deeds or a some act of will. When you were a baby, you were still you, even though it was long before you could think, do or have any will at all.

The things that happen to you, don't make you, you. There was a *you* before those things happened. One day you may be a young parent plunging your face into your child's hair and drinking in their scent, then, a middle aged person crying as you bury your father, or a wise elder sitting on your verandah sipping a cup of tea. You will still be you. Your identity is embedded within you but your identity is hard to define.

As I stood there, crying while the old lady asked me who I was, I was sorry that I couldn't give her a clear answer. Even as I squeezed out my response, I knew that it was not adequate. My grief came from a place deeply hidden away even from myself. A feeling of shared humanity and a profound sense that whatever happens to one person, happens to us all. I couldn't put this into words, even if I tried. When she asked me "who are you?", probably, my most honest answer would have been, "I don't know".

Once we take the leap of faith and decide to accept the Resurrection and the story of the Paschal Mystery, we too find ourselves like the sweet old lady. We see Jesus, who acts and lives a life unlike anybody else who has ever lived. Not only does he claim to speak with authority about who we are, who God is, and our ultimate destiny. But unlike anybody else who has ever lived, he is raised from the dead. How can we not gasp "who are you?"

Like the Auschwitz survivor, we are not asking for His name or His job or His life story. We are asking about the fundamental nature of his identity. And like me when confronted with the Auschwitz survivor's question, probably the best answer is, "I don't know".

Who Is Jesus? How to answer the Question

In chapter 3, I introduced the metaphor of the path of logic, the creek of uncertainty and the leap of faith. We have been following this path of reason and logic (*logos*) through the bush, but sometimes the path seems to have come to an end facing a creek. In our quest for meaning, sometimes reason fails. When that happens, we have had to make a leap of faith. We have to leap across the creek of uncertainty to continue or journey.

When we made the leap on the question of the existence of God and meaning in the universe, it was comforting to find reason waiting for us on the other side. It gave us a kind of certainty. But this time, when we take the leap and declare that Jesus was raised from the dead, there is no certainty. Instead, we are confronted with the complex question, "Who is Jesus of Nazareth?"

Before we begin to address this question, I want to make an important point. It's perfectly reasonable and life-giving to take the leap of faith and give our hearts to the teaching of Jesus and the Paschal Mystery. We could make this place on the far side of the creek our home and live a full and meaningful life here.

But I'm not going to do that. The question of who Jesus is drives us. It's like a goad that forces us on a very different and difficult path. So, I will make this bank of the creek a base camp, not a home. We can always come back to it (and in my life I often do), but let's respond to the goad. It drives us through a tangled path and it is up hill all the way. Some people have made the journey using a leap of faith but for me, I need my reason.

The first Christians, those who gave their hearts to Jesus' message and His story, wrestled with the question of His identity for over 400 years. They argued, fought, and even killed each other over it. It's a long and fairly sordid story. A cautionary tale of the highest order but eventually they came to what is generally considered the only reasonable answer. In this chapter, I'm going to use a little shortcut so that nobody gets killed.

Whatever answer we come up with to the question about the identity of Jesus, there are a few basic things that we must accept. The first is that, in essence, a person's identity is always mysterious and unknowable, even to themselves. Therefore, every answer must be inadequate. Secondly, we are not questioning the identity of Jesus just to stretch our intellectual legs, we are on a quest for meaning in life. If we have taken the leap to accept the teaching of Jesus and the Paschal Mystery, then that must be our primary interpretative lens. Any answer that we come up with about the identity of Jesus must not contradict this foundational metaphor.

In Chapter 4, I used the analogy of the spotlights and the statue. It's as if the source of all meaning is a statue in the night. All our symbols, stories and metaphors are spotlights that illuminate part of the statue from different angles but, because of its transcendent nature, they can't cast light on all of it. For Christians, the Paschal Mystery is the main spotlight that enables us to see the statue. Any other light that we turn on must illuminate the same statue (from a different angle), or else we can discount it as pointing in the wrong direction and not relevant to our quest for meaning. This gives us a means of testing the possible answers to the question, "Who is Jesus?"

Let me give you an example. Jen (J'ma) is proof reading this book. I believe that J'ma loves me and I have given my heart to that belief. If someone were to ask me, why J'ma was proofreading this book, and suggest that she was trying to make it worse, so that no one would read it, I would discount that interpretation because it conflicts with my belief that she loves me.

In the same way, once we've decided to give our hearts to the Paschal Mystery, any answer to the question, "Who is Jesus?" Cannot contradict central message of the Paschal Mystery, which is that the life, death and resurrection of Jesus reveals who we are, and the ultimate meaning and purpose of life.

Who Is Jesus? Five possible responses

Throughout Christian history there are broadly five possible answers to the question. We're going to look at all five, but let's take the first two together.

i) Jesus was a wonderful man. A kind of *Bhodisattva* (in Buddhism, someone who has achieved enlightenment but continues to be reborn to help others). He was so holy that God raised him from the dead.

ii) Jesus was an ordinary man. But God, in an act of sheer grace, gave him a profound insight into reality and vindicated this insight by raising him from the dead.

Both of these answers seem quite reasonable but they stumble over the Paschal Mystery. It makes the resurrection of Jesus either something he earned or else a special gift granted only to him. If we accept either of these answers, we have no reason to believe that the Paschal Mystery has any universal significance. Jesus rose from the dead, so what? The world, the universe, and most importantly, me, are still on a dead end road. And death makes everything meaningless.

Many Christians get out of this pickle by positing a heavenly abode beyond this world where we all go when we die. The idea is that Jesus' resurrection somehow opens the gates to Heaven and allows us ordinary folk to get in.

There are many problems with this. Firstly, the Paschal Mystery does not allow for a dualistic world view (Where heaven is spiritual and superior while earth is physical and inferior). There is absolutely nothing in the life, teaching, death and resurrection of Jesus that even hints that the material world is inferior to the spiritual. According to Jesus, the Kingdom of God is here now. It includes and embraces all of creation – everything is good and sacred. This is reinforced by the resurrection. Jesus didn't turn into a ghost or "go to heaven". His body didn't decompose. It was resurrected into a different form but it was absolutely physical. I'll say more about Heaven and Hell in Chapter 15.

Let's move on to the third possible answer. This is also reasonable and was quite popular in the ancient world, but not many people take this very seriously now.

iii) Jesus was God. The supreme being, the ultimate ground and horizon of reality, became a human being. Like an author who writes himself into his own story. No matter what happens to the author within the story, the author still exists above and beyond that level of reality. In the same way, God, who cannot die, cannot be held by death.

This too contradicts the central message of the Paschal Mystery. If God wrote Herself into the story and then rose from the dead, we could respond with, "So What?" Why should anyone believe that we too will be raised from death. As an Author, I can raise any of my characters from the dead. I don't need to write myself into the story to do that. Just because the Paschal Mystery applies to God, why should it apply to the rest of us.

The fourth possible answer is iv) Jesus was not just a child of God, he was *The Son of God*. Something less than God, but more than human. The best known example of this idea is the *Arian* heresy. In which Jesus, God's son, was created by God and sent down to Earth to reveal God's message and then die and rise again.

But if God's first begotten Son should experience the Paschal Mystery, why should that be relevant to humanity? According to this possible answer, Jesus wasn't really human in the way we are. He was more than human (but less than God). So why should the resurrection of this superior being have any impact on our ultimate meaning? Also, there is nothing in the teaching of Jesus that even hints that Jesus thought that his identity as Son of God was any different to our relationship as sons and daughters of God.

All the above answers to the question "Who is Jesus" undermine the Paschal Mystery as the central metaphor for meaning in life. When we take a leap of faith and declare that we believe in the Paschal Mystery, we are claiming that the life, death and resurrection of Jesus is the supreme revelation of the nature of reality and the meaning of life. All of the above answers, make the life, death and resurrection of Jesus a side issue. Not relevant to us and not applicable to the whole of creation.

And so, after 400 years of struggle, the followers of Jesus came up with the only answer that didn't undercut the primary message of the Paschal Mystery. They expressed it in a form of words that we still hold today.

Jesus is fully human and fully divine.(Council of Chalcedon: 451)
Of one essence (homoousios) with the Father
and through whom all things were made.(Council of Nicea: 325)

This answer doesn't contradict the Paschal Mystery, but it sure as hell leaves us scratching our heads. It seems completely illogical.

It's as if we've followed the path of reason up the hill and come to a tangle of blackberries. You can be forgiven if you decide to shrug your shoulders and head back to base camp, or even declaring that the original leap of faith was a mistake.

But don't despair. The path doesn't end here. We can get through the blackberries and reach the top of the hill and I promise you, the view from the top is really worth it. But we will need to develop a different way of knowing. We will have to tread the path of the mystics

The Mystical Way Of Knowing

We have taken a leap of faith, and decided to tentatively believe that Jesus was raised from the dead and that the Paschal Mystery is the key to the meaning of life. We jumped over the creek of uncertainty and tried to use our reason on the other side. But we've hit a tangle of blackberries on the other side of the creek:

The only answer to the question of who Jesus is that does not undermine the Paschal mystery is:
Jesus Christ: Fully human, fully divine
Of one being with the Father
Through whom all things were made
And this seems to makes no sense.

If you've stuck with me after that, congratulations. You must really want to find meaning in life. How on earth can we make any sense of this? This statement seems to fly in the face of all reason because it seems to completely contradict itself. A thing can't be and not be at the same time. The Jewish carpenter from Galilee who was born sometime around 4BC, can't be divine, can't be the one through whom all things were made. We simply cannot reason our way through this.

There are a couple things we need to get straight before we push on. The first is to remind ourselves that we are not using literal language here. This is symbolic language because we are attempting to talk about things that are transcendent, completely beyond our thoughts, our words and our experience. I don't know who I am. How can I know who Jesus is?

The second is that if we are to get through this tangle of blackberries, we will need a completely different way of knowing. So far we have got here through reason with a couple of leaps of faith. But this is pretty much as far as we can go using that method. To get further we need to tread the ways of the mystics. This mystical way of knowing is the most important part of this chapter. This is why we have continued the journey beyond the Paschal Mystery. To fully grasp the meaning of life, we need to develop this new, mystical way of knowing.

Now I'm no great mystic, I promise you. If you lit a candle and asked me to chant mantras, I'd last about 45 seconds before I'd start thinking about the football, or what I want to eat for lunch. But the good news is that you don't have to be a great mystic or even a good mystic to get through the blackberries. You can be a crap mystic and still get through. I think I'm probably the shittest mystic I know, and I get through. So can you.

The mystical way of knowing is actually pretty simple. You can't reason your way through this stuff. You mustn't break it down and rationalise it. You've got to listen to it, sit with it and let it seep into your heart. As you read this section, you'll need to do that repeatedly. You'll need to spend time sitting and not thinking. Spend time listening to the silence and marvelling. Then, you might get a glimpse of what this is about. It won't be clear. And you won't be able to describe what you see in words. You'll just experience a different form of knowing.

Once you've developed the knack of mystical knowing, then you'll find that it comes quite easily to you. You'll be able to slip into it as easily as you slip into rational thought or humming a tune. But it takes a fair bit of practice and if you haven't been raised with meditation or prayer or any other form of mysticism, you may find it hard to break old rationalist habits.

This mystical way is not unique to Christianity. It seems to have popped up in just about every great religious tradition. Buddhists, Daoists, Hindus, Muslims and Jews all have a mystical tradition and they all seem to have been developed in isolation from each other. And yet, their insights are surprisingly congruent (but not the same). I believe that this mystical way of knowing is just as real and as inherent to the human condition as is reason. It's just that culturally, we in the west de-emphasise it and exalt reason.

So, let's begin with some safe rational steps. Remember I told you that if God exists, She must be both Transcendent and Immanent? That if God, the uncaused cause, created the universe out of nothing (*ex nihilio*) then the only "stuff" that She could have used was Herself. Therefore we have these two aspects of God. The transcendent first cause, and the immanent divine essence that is the building block of all that is.

A hundred years or so before Jesus was born, Jewish philosophy was using a Greek word to describe this immanent aspect of God. The word was *logos*.

We've talked about *logos* before. It's the rational, argumentative part of our belief system. In Jewish philosophy *logos* was a kind of rational principle. An idea or a plan. God's plan, God's idea. Using the metaphor of a novelist, it's as if God had an idea for a story and created the story in Her own head before She wrote it down. But the divine Novelist doesn't need a pen and paper, She creates the whole story inside Her mind, and that's where all of creation exists.

Because God is eternal and therefore not subject to time, there could never be a time before the idea. The idea of the story came out of God but there was never "a time" when it didn't exist. This *logos*, this idea, this plan of God is as eternal as God Herself.

Jesus called the Transcendent part of God, Father and the first Christian mystics followed his lead. They talked of the Father as the creator, the one utterly beyond us out of which the *Logos* (the immanent part of God) emanated. They called the *Logos*, The Son.

About 60 years after the death of Jesus, the Christian community in Ephesus, gathered together the stories and sermons of the last apostle, John. And put them together in the literary form we call a gospel.

The purpose of this gospel was not to tell the story or record what Jesus taught. It was to answer the question: Who is Jesus? This is how they started their work...

> *In the beginning was the Logos*
> *And the Logos was with God*
> *And the Logos was God*
> *All things were made through him*
> *And without him was not anything that was made...*
> *And the Logos became flesh dwelt among us (Jn 1: 1-3,14)*

So the early Christians considered Jesus to the *Logos* made flesh. In other words, the immanent part of God, in human form.

How can this be? If we want to make our way through the blackberries, we'll need to access the mystical way of knowing.

> *Go find a place to sit, where you won't be disturbed. Look out at the trees, the grass, the hills, the clouds. Listen to the sound of the birds, feel the wind and sun on your skin. That's the immanent aspect of God. You're sitting on God. You're hearing God. Your breathing God. Let that sink in to you until the clouds part briefly and then you'll see it. You'll feel it. You'll know it.*

Everything exists within God. We are characters in a story written by God. Everything we see touch, smell or feel is part of a setting that exists within God.

Of course, Jesus is fully human and fully divine. So are the hills, the trees, the birds, the clouds, the stars... so are you!

11

Trinity: The Nature Of Reality

The Holy Spirit

In the previous chapter we looked at the early mystical tradition of Christianity and how they came to describe Jesus as the divine *Logos* that is present in all of creation. In this Chapter we are going to look at how the mystics went on from this insight to describe the Holy Spirit and create the metaphor of the Trinity. The idea that there is only one God but this God exists as three *persons* (Father, Son and Holy Spirit).

For us to grasp the concept of the Trinity, we have to engage in a similar mystical method that the early Christian mystics used. It will not be easy. We need to spend time in silence and contemplation, letting the thoughts and feelings percolate within us.

In this chapter, I'm trying to summarise what the early mystics came up with through their alternative way knowing. But you cannot just take another person's mystical insights and declare them true. If you did that, you would run the risk of becoming dogmatic and taking things too literally. To truly grasp these insights, you will have to do the mystical work for yourself.

Let's go back over some of the things we've already considered and then explore the idea of The Holy Spirit. From there we will look at the various ways people have described the Trinity metaphor and then look at the ways the metaphor has been interpreted.

Throughout the first centuries of Christianity, men and women devoted their lives to prayer and contemplation, and it was those people who led the debates about the nature of Jesus. Christian mystics believed in an eternal, transcendent, divine creator who created the universe out of nothing.

Remember, we don't know if there is a first cause but if there is, then this cause must have created the universe out of nothing (otherwise She is not the first cause). If there was nothing, then the creator must have used Herself as the building blocks for all that exists. That's why we can say that God is immanent in everything, such as stars, a sunset, a forest glade and us, because She used herself to create everything.

So the first Christian mystics proposed an immanent, eternal, divine *Logos*. The idea or vision or blueprint of the creator, embedded in the physical universe. Jesus was seen as the *incarnation* (enfleshment) of this eternal *Logos*.

Christians have traditionally named the creator as Father and the logos as Son. But remember these are just words. Metaphors for something completely beyond our language. We could just as easily call them mother and daughter. The metaphor works just as well (possibly even better).

But the Father/Son metaphor wasn't the only aspect of God that Jesus talked about. Jesus often referred to a reality called "The Holy Spirit". According to Jesus, The Holy Spirit animates us and moves through us, calling us into union with God.

Because this teaching, from the earliest days of the Church, Christians were Baptised (meaning, immersed) into the Father, Son and The Holy Spirit. The early mystics therefore had to wrestle with a new set of questions. Who or what is this Spirit that we are immersed in? How does the Spirit within us relate to the transcendent Creator and the immanent *logos*? Let's have a look at their answers.

There is something fundamentally different about any conscious being and an inanimate one. So the mystics proposed that the way God was immanent in humans was different from the way God was immanent in rocks or stars. There is a divine spark deep in the human heart that causes us to yearn for meaning and calls us into union with God. This is what Jesus meant when he spoke about the Holy Spirit.

Remember in Chapter Two, we defined God as the ultimate source of meaning in the Universe. God is the context and frame of reference which gives meaning to everything. Therefore the human yearning for meaning is in fact a yearning for God. According to the mystics, our desire for meaning is driven by The Holy Spirit. It's as if one part of God is within us, dragging us towards unity with the other parts of God. (Remember I'm speaking poetically and metaphorically here.)

But it's not just our yearning for meaning which is driven by The Holy Spirit. According to the mystics, all our yearnings are in fact a yearning for God and all our yearnings are driven by the Holy Spirit.

We are finite beings who long for the infinite. We yearn for meaning, for love, for belonging, for beauty, and for goodness. All this longing is a manifestation of our deepest desire, which is to be united with God because, according to Christianity, God is the ultimate source of meaning, goodness, beauty and love. As Augustine of Hippo says, *"You made us for yourself, oh Lord, and our hearts are restless until they rest in you"*.

Of course, it's possible to break up all the yearnings of our heart and analyse them as products of genetics, hormones and evolution. But as Aristotle said, *"The whole is greater than the sum of its parts"*. The yearning in our heart is greater than these little desires. There is a greater emergent reality that transcends our simple science based explanations of the various parts.

For example, imagine trying to explain a great work of art, by simply analysing the paint flecks, brush strokes and pigments. All these things give us information about the artwork and how it was created, but the work of art is more than its component parts.

To appreciate the art, we must let go of our desire to break down and micro-analyse it. We must open ourselves to the whole of the artwork. Experience it. Let it move us. Let it speak to our heart. That's what it is like to find meaning in life. We can never find meaning by breaking things down. We must encounter and experience things as a whole, if we are to find meaning.

The Metaphor of The Trinity

In the previous section we looked at how the first Christian mystics talked about God using three aspects; the transcendent creator who is utterly beyond us (Father), the immanent *Logos*, present in all creation but especially in Jesus of Nazareth (Son) and the Holy Spirit within us. The Father, Son, and The Holy Spirit. These are the three persons of *The Trinity*. This is the second great metaphor of Christian tradition.

Remember metaphors are a form of symbolic language. They are not meant to be explained, they are meant to be interpreted. The Trinity doesn't define God. God can't be defined because God, if She exists, She must be transcendent.

Throughout Christian history, there have been many attempts to illustrate The Trinity but all of them are imperfect. Here are a few attempts that I find helpful as I wrestle with this metaphor. None of these attempts can be conquered rationally. This is where you need to do the mystical work for yourself. Each of them need to be sat with and meditated on, allowing the insight to seep into your heart and soul.

1. The first chapter of Genesis tells us that God looked upon all He created and saw that it was very good. So we have the divine Father gazing lovingly at the divine *Logos* enfleshed in creation. We have the divine *logos* receiving this loving gaze and reflecting it back. And the loving gaze itself is a third being, The Holy Spirit.

2. When I was in primary school, I was taught that the Father loves the Son and the Son loves the Father and the love is so great, it becomes a third person.

3. The English word "person" comes from the Greek word *prosopon* which means face or mask. In Greek theatre, the actors would use a mask that sometimes had a little megaphone attached to it.

When an actor would play a character, they would take the *prosopon* and speak through it so the audience could hear and understand what part they were playing. This is another metaphor to help understand the Trinity metaphor. God speaks through these three different *proposon*. The Father, the Son and the Spirit.

But we use the word "person" to describe all of us. I'm a person and so are you. We are the masks of God. Hidden behind everyone and everything, is the eternal, transcendent God who is the ultimate source of meaning in the world.

4. C.S. Lewis used another analogy. He said a line is a being with only one dimension, length. If you add a second dimension (width), you can have an infinite amount of lines that can create an infinite number of shapes; squares, rectangles, triangles etc. If you add a further dimension (height) you can create a whole new class of object like cubes and pyramids. We can image one square consisting of four lines, or a single cube consisting of six squares.

In the same way, in the human dimension we have many persons and each person seems to be a separate being. In the divine dimension, there can be more than one person in a being. There's room in the Divine cube for everybody.

5. The Greek mystics described the Trinity as a dance. If you saw two people dancing, there are the two dancers, and the dance itself, which is different from the dancers but can't be

separated from them. All reality is a Divine dance where the dancer and the dance are separate but deeply united.

We can say that our purpose is to join in this great divine dance and that is how we find meaning. In the metaphor of the dance, The Holy Spirit is the music, resonating in our hearts and inviting us to join in this wonderful celebration. I'll come back to this metaphor several times as we continue our quest.

Remember, these are all just ways of explaining a metaphor, a way of trying to understand something that is not understandable. This is heady stuff and the more we think about it, the less sense it seems to make. But the more we pray about it, the *more* sense it seems to make. This is the different form of knowing that the mystics use, and we must learn it, if we are to grow.

Some Interpretations of The Trinity

Like all symbolic language, the metaphor of the Trinity can't be fully explained. It can only be interpreted. There are countless ways of interpreting this metaphor. I'm only going to discus six interpretations in this book. What does the Trinity metaphor tell us about God and the nature of reality?

Around the turn of the fifth century, Augustine of Hippo was trying to write a book about the Trinity. He was struggling. One night he had a dream. He dreamt that he was walking along a beach and came upon a small boy who had dug three holes in the sand.
"What are you doing?" Augustine asked.
The boy smiled enthusiastically. "I've dug these three holes, and now I'm going to empty the ocean into them."
Augustine laughed. "Son, you can't empty the sea into your three little holes."
Suddenly, the boy stood up straight and pierced Augustine with a knowing look. "And you, my Son, can never understand the Trinity."

I'm not sure how true the story is but it leads us to the first major interpretation of the Trinity.

i) The Trinity is a permanent reminder of the transcendence of God. The old man who sits on a cloud and sends thunderbolts from heaven, is not a Trinitarian God. It's a mental image which may be popular for children but it's not Christian, it's not philosophically sound, and it's not helpful for adults.

ii) The Trinity resists any type of literal interpretation. You simply cannot take the Trinity literally. It forces us to think metaphorically not literally.

iii) The metaphor seems to defy our human reason so it forces us to move beyond our reason and drives us towards mysticism. We have to experience God in our hearts, not just in our minds. We have to experience meaning in our lives, not just in our thoughts. The meaning that we are questing for is not a puzzle and it can never be solved. Karl Rahner, probably the greatest Catholic theologian of the 20th century said, "Christians of the future will either be mystics or they will not exist" (Theol. Invent. XX, 149).

iv) The Trinity metaphor tells us that God is more than a person. Many people say that they don't believe in a personal God because they think that a transcendent God cannot be a person. But they then often fall into the trap of imagining God as being less than a person, impersonal. The Trinity offers us a way of imagining God as being greater than a person. God is not just one person, God is three.

v) The metaphor of the Trinity tells us that God is not outside of the universe. Not a passive observer or an external judge. God is completely engaged and immersed in the universe. There is no division or distinction between the divine and the natural. That only exists in our heads. It's all one. One God.

vi) The Trinity metaphor tells us that the fundamental nature of God is a relationship. Not an exclusive relationship between two, but an inclusive relationship based on three. The heart of this relationship is Love. God is Love.

Because God created everything, then all reality exists within God. If God is Trinity, then all reality must share this *Trinitarian* nature.

We exist within one great love relationship. A relationship that's dynamic, flowing, developing. A relationship that includes everything from the simplest bacteria to the highest intellect. From the smallest sub-atomic particle to the largest galaxy. Everything is within this Trinity. Everything is God. Everything is a manifestation of Love.

In mainstream Christianity, The Trinity metaphor is the most important depiction of the nature of God. but it also depicts the fundamental nature of all reality, because all reality exists within God.

All interpretations of the Trinity require a mystical way of knowing. You can't simply understand them. You're not going to get through the tangle of blackberries by thinking.

You will have to sit with these interpretations in silent reflection. Don't try to wrestle them to the ground with your reason. They are more like poetry than prose. More like music than a mathematical formula. Let them soak into you.

Eventually these interpretations of the Trinity metaphor will become part of the fabric of your life and your life will have meaning.

God is Love

When I was teaching, I had a lesson plan for year tens. It was designed to help kids reflect on the Trinity and introduce them to the mystical way of knowing.

I would begin by asking them to write down the things they had been taught about God. Then I would get them to call them out and I would write them on the board. I'd do this, because often the stuff they had been taught about God was bullshit and I needed to sort through it. So things like, "God is an old man on a cloud" became "God is utterly beyond our understanding," and "God never dies."

The edited list on the board was usually something like this:
God is all powerful.
God understands everything.
Everything came from God.
God holds the universe together.
God is our origin and our destiny.
God gives life meaning.
God never dies.
God is beyond our understanding.
God cannot be proved.
God cannot be controlled.
We exist within God.
God forgives our failings.
We can trust God.

Once the board was full or the kids had run out of ideas, I'd get them to put the heading "God is Love" into their books. We'd talk a bit about where the idea comes from, then I'd tell them to copy the statements from the board into their books under the heading, but wherever the word "God" is written, replace it with the word "Love."

In their books, they would write something like this....

<u>God is Love</u>
Love is all powerful.
Love understands everything.
Everything came from Love.
Love holds the universe together.
Love is our origin and our destiny.
Love gives life meaning.
Love never dies.
Love is beyond our understanding.
Love cannot be proved.
Love cannot be controlled.
We exist within Love.
Love forgives our failings.
We can trust Love.

It was fun to listen as the kids realised what they were doing. Sometimes they'd laugh as the insight kicked in, or maybe resist the ideas and argue, or sometimes even gasp.

After we'd talk about it a bit, I would finish with this:

What sets Christianity apart is not so much what we believe about God, but what we believe about Love.

Love is not a wishy-washy emotion, or a blind twist of evolution. Love is the infinite ground and horizon of all reality, embedded within the finite universe.

God is Love, and whoever abides in love, abides in God.

I began this book by defining God as the ultimate source of all meaning in the Universe. Now, through the metaphor of the Trinity, Christians define God as love. Therefore love is the ultimate source of meaning in the universe. The meaning and purpose of human life is experienced by loving and being loved, because God is love.

For the rest of this book, whenever you see the word "God" you can read the word "love" because God is love. When I tell you to trust God, I'm telling you to trust love. When I tell you that you have to throw yourself off the table into the arms of God and hope that She catches you, I'm telling you to throw yourself into the arms of love. When I tell you that death does not have the last word, God does. I'm telling you that Love has the last word.

When the mystics talk about the Trinity as a Divine dance, they are talking about a Love dance. Loving is like dancing. You can't concentrate on your dance moves or break the dance down into little pieces. You just have to let yourself go and move to the music.

Let yourself go, and live in Love. All reality is One God; One Love; Father, Son and Spirit. Three persons madly in Love with each other and passionately in love with you.

An Example and a Parable

Remember, the Trinity is not a literal description of the nature of God, it is a form of symbolic language to express something that is fundamentally inexpressible. If it is a description of anything at all, the Trinity describes how humans encounter God. It was born out of spiritual experience and I believe it's best understood experientially, not rationally.

Here is an experience of Trinity from my own life. About ten years ago, J'ma and I were driving through eastern Victoria on a holiday. We saw a sign pointing down a dirt road "The Nargun's Den". When I was young, I read a book called the Nargun and the Stars and I loved it. So when I saw the sign, I convinced her to go on a detour to see this place. We had no idea what it was going to be. It may have been a shop for all I knew.

We arrived at the place and there was nothing around except a sign saying "Nargun's Den". The bush was scrubby and dry and we had to walk about a hundred metres or so down a hill. We emerged into a little dale with temperate rainforest. Old gum trees broke through the canopy of ancient tree ferns that clustered around a billabong. On the other side of the pond, a cave opened out into water, blocking access. The only sound was that of the moist air dripping from fern fronds onto the surface of the pond. Even the birds seemed silent.

We sat together on a rock neither of us speaking. The beauty, stillness, the peace, was breathtaking. After a while, J'ma whispered, "I feel like I want to cry".

I'm now going to ruin that experience by putting shitty human words on it. We encountered God, immanent and profoundly present in that little rainforest billabong (*Logos*). Our hearts sang as we knew we belonged (The Holy Spirit). But at the same time, there was a yearning within us. This wonderful billabong, somehow pointed away from itself to a transcendent Other that we could glimpse but not grasp (The Father).

Let's now take it a step further and look at this through a parable.

Two parents are dancing at a party. Their teenaged son is sitting watching from the side and the mother calls the son to join in.

The son scowls, "Dancing is silly," he thinks, "Besides, I'm too old to dance with Mum and Dad. Dancing with my parents is lame." But deep in his heart, he remembers a time when he would have danced. He remembers the joy of abandon and trust, and yearns for it.

Years pass, and the parents grow old and the boy becomes a man with children of his own. They attend the wedding of the man's daughter and there on the dance floor, the old couple once more get up to dance.

The son's eyes are filled with tears. His mother looks across and beckons to him.

And this time, he comes, and they dance. The boy/man no longer cares about silliness, or what others may think, he is just happy to share this moment with the two people who have loved him into life.

The Holy Spirit is within us, calling us to get up and dance, to let go of our egos and our need for approval. Just get up and start moving to the music. Be part of the divine dance.

We've struggled past the tangle of blackberries, now, kids. We've got to the top and the vista opens up before us. Now we just have to look at it. Our entire quest for meaning is just a matter of reflecting on and interpreting the two great metaphors: the Paschal Mystery and the Trinity. The Paschal

Mystery is the pattern of life and the Trinity is the nature of God and reality. Contemplating these two metaphors enable us to wrestle with the nature of ultimate reality and the meaning and purpose of life.

I could end this book here. You could complete the quest on your own by simply developing your capacity for mystical knowing and reflecting on the metaphors of the Paschal Mystery and Trinity. But just like when you started riding a bike and your Dad ran behind holding onto your seat to keep you upright, Grandpa's going to hang around for a little bit longer to show you the process.

> *We did not ask for this room,*
> *or this music;*
> *we were invited in.*
> *Therefore,*
> *because the dark surrounds us,*
> *let us turn our faces toward the light.*
> *Let us endure hardship*
> *to be grateful for plenty.*
> *We have been given pain*
> *to be astounded by joy.*
> *We have been given life*
> *to deny death.*
> *We did not ask for this room,*
> *or this music.*
> *But because we are here,*
> *let us dance.*
>
> Stephen King

12

Love

What is Love?

Last chapter, we used faith, reason and our new-found mystical way of knowing to declare that God is love. The obvious follow up question then, is "What is love?"

When I was a kid, I used to think that love was an extreme form of liking. "I like cricket, but I *love* football." "I like lizards, but I *love* birds." I'll come back to this idea later because there is some truth to it, but even then, I knew it really doesn't work as a definition of love. I knew that there were people who liked me, but didn't love me. And now as an adult, I've discovered that many times I have loved someone deeply without actually liking them. It would seem that love and liking may be related but they are not the same.

Some people talk of love as a feeling. The warm gooey feeling we get in our heart that causes us to say, "Ooh I love you." Again, there is some truth to this but having raised three children that I love very much, I can tell you with absolute confidence that a lot of the time, my love was expressed with no warm gooey feelings at all. After a night where the baby woke me up three times, I would feed her breakfast out of pure love, but there were no feelings attached to it. So love must be more than just an emotion.

Some say that love is what we do. That true love expresses itself in concrete actions for another person. It's certainly true that merely saying "I love you" to another person or feeling the emotion, without ever lifting a finger to help them is not genuine love. But there is more to love than just what we do. When my mother made me a sandwich for lunch, it was an act of love, but when the local cafe makes me a sandwich, there is very little love involved. The actions are the same, but only one is an act of love. So love must be more than just what we do.

People often ask the question, "Is love a feeling or an action?" I think the answer is neither. Fire causes both heat and light, but neither heat nor light is fire. Fire is something else. Similarly, love causes deep emotions and it leads to powerful acts both great and small, but neither the acts nor the emotions are love. Love is something else.

The standard theological definition of love is *"Willing the good for another for that other's sake."* In other words, an act of will that seeks what is good for another person even if we get nothing in return. This isn't a bad definition of love. It certainly encompasses both the emotional and the action elements of love discussed above but here I must dare to sheepishly disagree with these more learned folk. I have two problems with the theological definition of Love.

The first problem is its emphasis on willing the good *for others*. Love should not *only* be applied to others. We also need to love ourselves. You are a person too, and you deserve the same love, care and respect that you give to everyone else. If you constantly sacrifice yourself for others you are basically exploiting yourself.

Jesus said to "love your neighbour as yourself". You can't do this if you don't love yourself. Jesus just assumed that His audience would love themselves because that is what a healthy person does.

The second problem I have with the theological definition is it's emphasis on the act of will. I fully accept that love requires an act of will but I don't think an act of will captures the whole reality of Love. It seems a little too bloodless for my liking. There's not enough emotion, passion, rage or joy. The theological definition emphasises the act of will but I think love is more than that.

So if love is more than emotion, more than actions, more than an act of will, then what is it? All these things are elements of love. Some of them seem necessary for love but none of them fully explain the reality. Is it possible to define love?

If Christians are correct and God is love, then Love must be transcendent. (From now on, when I'm talking about transcendent Love, I'm going to capitalise it.) Love must be therefore beyond our understanding and it must be impossible to simply lock Love into a simple definition. Every attempt to describe Love must be imperfect, just as every attempt to describe God is imperfect.

If Love is transcendent, then we find ourselves falling back to the metaphor of the statue in the night, that I discussed when referring to God. We can shine a spotlight on the statue from one angle and this would illuminate some parts of the statue, but it would also cast large parts of the statue into shadow, making them invisible. We can't see the whole statue at once. So let's try to shine a few lights on this wonderful statue of Love, and see what the lights reveal.

Four Loves and More- *Storge* and *Philia*

Towards the end of his life, C.S. Lewis wrote a wonderful book called "The Four Loves". It was based on the idea that in Greek (which is the language the New Testament was written in) there are four words for Love, not just one. These are; *Storge, Philia, Eros* and *Agape*. In this chapter I'm going to use these four words as spotlights to illuminate a part of the transcendent statue that is Love.

Storge is family love. It is the love of parents, brothers and sisters. Lewis, portrays *storge* in a simple image, a litter of puppies being nursed by a mother dog. *Storge* is comfortable and familiar like your favourite pair of slippers. It grows out of spending long periods of time together. It is not just found in families. We encounter it in workplaces, classrooms and sporting teams. *Storge* is the love we feel for our tribe.

There are many wonderful aspects of *storge*. It's not earned. If we are ugly or pretty, smart or stupid, hard working or lazy, it doesn't matter. If we are part of the family, part of the group, part of the tribe, we are loved. *Storge* is the most universal of loves. Not only does it appear in other species, but it can also cross the divide between species. Humans and their companion animals and even between the animals themselves.

But every human construct of Love has shadows. Here are some of the shadow sides of *storge*.

Love of our tribe can lead to exclusion of those we see as "other". Tribalism is often a synonym for racism. *Storge* can become insular, distrusting and resentful.

The doting Love of a parent can become controlling. One of the hardest things about parenting, is letting your child grow up and move on with their life.

Storge can also become stifling. Families and tribes each have a unique culture and the pressure to conform to this culture can sometimes stifle the growth and development of the individual members. A family whose culture is sporting and physical, may resent a member who begins to engage in music or intellectual pursuits. A tribe whose culture is deeply secular may resent a member who pursues spirituality and quests for meaning.

The next type of Love Lewis discusses is *philia*, the love we feel for a friend. We often use the word friend to include anyone we know or get along with reasonably well. But as we get older, we find that friendship is a rare and beautiful thing. When I was at school, I had lots of people I called friends, but I can count on the fingers of one hand, the true friends I've had in my life.

There's a special meeting of hearts and minds between friends. It doesn't matter if you see each other every day or once a year. You are bound together by shared values, interests and something more. I can't explain it, but having a true friend is a wonderful gift and it's very sad that many people in our society do not have true friends. They have only acquaintances and family.

But *philia* too has its shadow side. Friendships can bind people to values and lifestyles that are unhealthy or even corrupt. Two criminals can become firm and fast friends, trusting each other and sharing their deepest thoughts. And together, they reinforce each other's criminal behaviour.

When I was teaching, I realised that the people whose company I most enjoyed were not necessarily the best people. In friendship, I value humour, wit and humility. There were many good and decent people at school who bored me shitless, while I found myself attracted to others who were not so good.

Many friendships are based on shared values, but sometimes those shared values are not good for us. If a person has taken a wrong path in life and decided to pursue power, pleasure, status or wealth, they may well find themselves surrounded by friends who share those values. These friendships can then become a powerful force that reinforces their unhealthy values.

If that person tried to look beyond the dead-end values of power, wealth, status and pleasure, it would probably cost them their friendships. Those friendships can trap them in a sad spiral of misery.

Four Loves and More- *Eros* and *Agape*

Eros is the third type of love that Lewis describes. We get the English word "erotic" from *eros* and because of this, many people mistakenly think that *eros* is just sex. This is wrong. Don't get me wrong, sex is bloody wonderful and if it's not wonderful for you, then you're doing it wrong. The vital ingredient to awesome sex is *eros*. *Eros* is romantic love. I have to tell you, being in love is one of the best things in the world!

> *I still remember my girlfriend in high school, sweet, pretty, putting her face so close to mine that our noses and foreheads touched. Then she'd laugh and say, "You've got three eyes."*

I know this story is silly but the memory still brings a smile to my face. There is nothing sexual about this memory but it is charged with *eros*.

Old bastards like me will often tell teenagers that they are too young to be in love. Don't be fooled. You can absolutely fall in love as a teenager and it's wonderful and terrifying and excruciating. The tragedy of teenage romantic love is that it usually doesn't last. One partner, usually ends up getting their heart broken. This is extremely painful, but it's not a bad thing. Everyone needs their heart broken in some way, otherwise they can't really love. I'll come back to this again in Chapter 14.

There are some people who don't believe in *eros*. They say that it is nothing more than lust and it fades away after a while and you can't expect to make it an important part of your life. For them, marriage is a contract of companionship, security and child-rearing. Nothing more.

This attitude was quite prevalent in your parents' generation when they were in their twenties. I suspect it developed because so many of their generation had heaps of sex with people they didn't love. Often, when those people got sick of the meaningless sex, they were willing to settle down (and settle for) anyone who would be a reasonable companion.

But *eros* is real. It's wonderful and magical and wild and irrepressible. It comes upon you unexpectedly and sweeps you away, turning your life upside down. When you fall in love everything is just dust compared to the one you're in love with. You'll burn down the whole world to get her.

Eros is like God. *Eros* has no regard for rules, human conventions or social niceties. It is a great consuming passion. In the Narnia chronicles, Aslan is Lewis' metaphor for God. In every book, somebody reminds the children that Aslan is not a tame lion, and neither is God.

She will seduce you, and sweep away all the things that the world considers important, and you will run after Her, enraptured, while those who think themselves worldly and wise tut and frown. but the worldly and wise have forgotten how to live. The only way to truly live is to throw your life away for Love. To climb up onto the table and throw yourself, arms open, into the air. Jesus said, "For whoever wants to save their life will lose it, but if you lose your life because of me (Love), you'll find it." (Matt 16: 25)

Eros is the spotlight that shines the brightest on Love. But because it's the brightest, it casts the deepest shadows. We can fall in love with people who are not good for us. Romantic relationships can often become profoundly abusive, physically, mentally and spiritually.

Eros can ruthlessly switch from one person to another. You can be deeply in love with someone one day and then, in the space of a few months, be passionately in love with someone else. This leads to terrible suffering and trauma for all those involved. But primarily for the one who is no longer loved.

Eros carries the constant danger of become selfish and insular. When *eros* is young and fresh, couples will often turn inwards, excluding the world. Most couples grow past that and reach out to the world again, but if they don't, the relationship will go into a death spiral of selfishness, hedonism and ultimately despair.

The ultimate shadow of *eros* is death. Eventually we all lose our lover. Even if the *eros* doesn't fade in one of us, or if the shadows don't become too great and overwhelm our love. Even if time and care don't wear down our *eros* into a bland form of *storge*, time will eventually break us. Eventually, one of us will stand at the grave of the other. Once you realise this, when you hold her in your arms and smell the fragrance of her hair, you'll cling even more tightly to her because you know that you only have a short time together.

The day after my mother died, my dad sat on the edge of his bed. His face had lost its usual ruddy hue. It was grey and wan like a tea towel that had been washed too many times.

He shook his head sadly and said with terrible finality, "My life is over, Son."

We sat on the bed together, side by side, holding hands, and I told him a story I got from Victor Frankl, a wonderful Jewish doctor who survived Auschwitz.

I told Dad, that one of them had to die first. "Either Mum would die and leave you like this, or else, you would die first and leave Mum grieving and broken. This pain you're feeling now is the last act of love that you are giving to her."

He looked up at me and nodded very seriously. I saw his lips tighten as if he were steeling himself. "Yes," he said. "I am bearing this pain so she doesn't have to."

In those twilight days of Dad's life, his memory was fading and you would have to tell him the same thing over and over again. But several times throughout the rest of his life, he told me, as if he had thought it all by himself, "I am bearing this grief so Mum doesn't have to."

This isn't *eros*, kids. This is *Agape*. *Agape* is willing what is best for the other, for the other's sake. It is selfless, it sacrifices itself for the benefit of others. Some say *Agape* is the queen of the loves but I think of it more as the health system that can protect us from the shadow sides of the other loves. When we will what is best for others for their own sake, then we are less likely to stifle our family members. We'd be more likely to take into account the feelings of others when we are in love. We would want our friends to become better people for their own sakes not just enjoying their company for what we can get out of them. *Agape* is a spotlight that shines across a vast area of Love's statue but its light is diffuse. Not sharp or intense. I think it's a mistake to define Love as *agape* alone but you can't have Love without *agape*.

In this section, I have only skimmed the surface of the complex issues around Love. Most of our lives are spent navigating treacherous waters between the bright light of the four loves and their deadly shadows. It's not an easy task and all of us run aground many times on our journey. I'll talk more about that in the next chapter.

But there are more than four spotlights on this transcendent statue. There are other loves. The Love of beauty, the Love of nature, the Love of music and art, the Love of work or activity. These are all elements of Love. They all have the capacity to make our souls sing, to add colour and iridescence to what could be a dull landscape. But all of these too, cast shadows.

Love is utterly beyond our understanding yet this is the Love that we have to live in. This is the Love that created the universe and it is what gives our lives meaning. It's transcendent, it can't be explained or understood with our rational minds. It can only be experienced with our hearts and our bodies and our souls. When you Love, your life has meaning, because God is Love.

13

Living in Love

Who Do You Love? Who Loves You?

In the previous chapter, we wrestled with the nature of Love. We discussed several different types of love but found each of them to have a shadow side. If the Trinity metaphor calls us to live lives that are immersed in Love, then successfully navigating these shadows becomes very important. In this chapter, I'm going to discuss some of the difficulties that we confront when we try to live in Love and make some suggestions to help you deal with them.

In the latter years of my teaching career, the students seemed to change. Many of them seemed more anxious, less relaxed, always worrying about their marks or their social standing. Whenever I'd get the opportunity, I'd tell them, "Guys, lighten up. It's just high school. None of this is important."

The kids would often react with a mixture of resistance and laughter. "Tell that to our parents."

"I will!" I'd say. "When you're on your death bed, the last thing you'll be thinking about is what mark you got in year 9 English."

"Yeah but if I don't get good marks, I won't get into my uni course."

"That's not so important," I'd say waving my hand and laughing.

Then the game would begin, kids shouting out all the reasons they've been told by teachers and parents for doing well in school, while I laugh and reply, "That's not important."

Eventually, one of the kids would say, "Well what is important!?"

Then I would suddenly stop laughing and pause, staring across the classroom intently. The kids would go quiet. Once the mood in the room had shifted, I'd say, "What is important is who you love, and who loves you."

When you're a teacher, you never know how much of what you teach sinks in. Most of it probably flies through to the keeper but I remember on day when I was preparing my Year 10 History class for the end of year exam, I had listed all the topics and key ideas on the board. We'd spent the whole lesson revising the course. At the end I waved my hand towards the board and said, "So, when you go home just study that and you'll be ready for the exam. That's the stuff that's most important."

Suddenly a sweet girl from the back row wagged her finger at me with a slight smile. "That's not important," she said. "What's important is who you love and who loves you."

At our best, our lives are an expanding circle of love. As time passes, you meet more and more people who you can love and who love you. Eventually, you are old and you can sit on your verandah and luxuriate in the glorious parade of all those you have loved and who have loved you. Life truly is wonderful.

But, I can hear you say, "Sure, Grandpa, it may seem wonderful for you but for me..." fill in the blank. My boyfriend has just dumped me, my teachers are awful, I have no friends in school, I'm fighting with my mum, my dad doesn't talk to me. The list can go on and on, can't it? The shit and misery of adolescence.

There's nothing I can write here, that can get you out of that shit, my darlings. I'm very sorry but adolescence is a difficult time and it's full of suffering. What I can tell you, though, is that everyone who has ever lived has also gone through this stage of life, and they got through it. Also, there are many, many people who have come out the other side and declared that they have had a wonderful life. You can too.

Surviving adolescence: Get Mel

In this section, I want to give you my "Adolescence Survival Kit". I used to teach this to my students in the last years of my teaching career in response to their growing anxiety. It's a hodge podge of ideas from various places and none of the ideas are mine. I called it "Get Mel".

Get Mel is an anagram. The first three letters represent three general attitudes that help you to have a healthy and happy life. The second three are things that you should try and do every day. These six things can work together to make adolescence bearable and your life wonderful.

G. E. T.: The first one is Gratitude. Humans are strange creatures. As soon as we have something good in our lives, we tend to take it for granted and start looking for the next good thing to have. By cultivating an attitude of gratitude we can protect ourselves from taking things for granted.

St. Francis of Assisi said, "If I keep looking, I will always find a reason to give thanks". That's what we must do. Last night I slept on a comfortable bed. The sunrise was beautiful this morning. My cup of tea was warm and sweet. The football season starts tomorrow. There are so many things to be grateful for in my life. Keep looking, and you'll always find a reason to be grateful.

Empathy is the second one. Empathy is a precursor to love. Empathy grows from imagining yourself in another person's situation. If you do that, then you'll find ways to do little things that may be very easy for you, but will enrich the lives of those around you. Once you start loving others, you'll find that they will start loving you. Keep imagining yourself in someone else's shoes, and you'll always find a reason to love.

The third attitude is <u>T</u>rust. Don't worry about the future and don't dwell on the bad things that have happened in the past. Your life is not just about you. You are a character in a divine novel and the Author of this novel loves you more than you can know. She will not let you down or abandon you.

Things will get hairy and you will suffer. You can't have a story without some adversity. But don't despair. The book of your life is long and you are only in chapter 8. Maybe chapter 8 is a sad chapter or maybe its happy, but the book will be wonderful because the Author loves you. Trust Her.

The next three things are the things you should try to do every day. <u>M. E. L.</u>: The first is <u>M</u>usic. Music is good for the soul. Sing, dance, play music, listen to music. The more music there is in your life, the more joy there will be. It doesn't matter what type of music, so long as you like it and it gives you joy.

When I was teenager, I didn't let myself enjoy the music I liked. I felt I had to like what everybody else liked. I missed out on a lot of joy because of that. Don't let anybody stop you from dancing or singing or listening to, or playing music.

<u>E</u>xercise is the second thing you should do every day. Do some physical activity each day. Run, play sport, work in the garden, make something. Of course, there may be days when it's too hot or it's rainy. Or maybe you feel sick one day. But try to do something physically challenging every day. You'll feel better for it.

The final thing to do each day is Laugh. Life is funny! There is always something to laugh at. Either you are about to do something stupid or maybe someone is about to say something funny. The more you laugh the more joy you will feel. There's always something funny just over the horizon. Don't miss the jokes in life by being too sad or serious. Keep your eyes peeled and your ears sharp. You will always find a reason to laugh.

I vividly remember Tuesday the 27th of April 2009. It was the middle of the worst week of my life. We had just found out on the previous Sunday that there was no more medical hope for my daughter, Emily. Her leukaemia was beyond cure. We didn't know that she was going die on the Friday but we all knew that the end was very close.

That evening, her sister, Hannah had brought home fried chicken from work and we were eating it. It was fatty and awful and I knew I was going to feel sick afterwards. Emily was a vegetarian but I convinced her that if she only ate the crust of the chicken, it wasn't eating meat. She decided to act as if she believed me. We all sat in Emily and Tim's lounge-room, eating disgusting chicken and talking. I can't remember what we were talking about, but I remember we were all laughing. I remember looking at Emily's face and watching the joy shining through it. I remember thinking, "My daughter is dying, my marriage is breaking up, I am failing as a husband and a father, my life is falling to pieces, but right now, here in this little lounge-room, I am filled with joy."

Never underestimate the power of laughter.

Gratitude, Empathy, Trust, Music, Exercise and Laughter are all important elements of living a healthy life but to find meaning in life, all these things must be embedded in Love, this mystical reality that we can experience but never understand.

Sin: Enemy of Love

If you've read this far into the book, you may be wondering why I haven't mentioned sin before now. For many people, when they think of religion or God, they immediately leap to the ideas of moral rules and sin. When I taught R.E. I only discussed sin in year 12. Despite what you may have heard from some Christians, it's simply not that important in the Gospel message.

Now you're probably thinking, "Hang on, Grandpa. Jesus talked about turning away from Sin, St. Paul talked about Sin a lot." And you'd be right... in fact it could be argued that the entire Christian message is a description of how to overcome Sin. Still... I stand by my original point. It's not that important. Let me explain...

Firstly, let's be clear about what Sin is, and what it is not. Sin is not the naughty things we do. That's not what Jesus or St. Paul meant when they were talking about Sin. That's just some bullshit we tell children because the idea of Sin is too complicated for them.

The gospels portray Jesus as a friend of sinners. He has no trouble at all with those who know they are sinners but with those who think they aren't and particularly with those who accuse and condemn others. Interestingly, the only people Jesus ever condemns are religious people.

The origin of the word "Sin" comes from archery. It literally means *"to miss the mark"*. When I was a kid, I went on a camp where they taught us archery. In my imagination, shooting an arrow was something that Robin Hood did. You just hold the bow, pull back the string and let the arrow fly.

Man! Was I in for a rude shock! That bloody arrow went everywhere except where I was aiming. As we left the range, the instructor laughed. "It's not easy is it?" He said. "But you did well. It takes years of practise to get good at archery and even then, you miss the target a lot of the time."

Can you remember the first time you kicked a football? I remember it hurt my foot and it barely went half way across the back yard. Kicking a football long and straight, requires a lot of practise. And even when I was playing football regularly, I missed my target more often than I hit it.

Imagine if one of your teammates misses a kick and then stops in the middle of the game, tears his jumper, beats his chest and weeps. Sounds a bit nuts, doesn't it? Yet that is what some (albeit well-meaning) religious people expect us to do.

What should you do when you miss a kick in the middle of a game? The polite thing to do, is put your hand up and apologise to your team mate. If you team mate is shitty, he may even give you a serve. You cop it. But you don't dwell on it. You get on with the game. When you get the ball next time, and you're trying to hit your target with a kick, you don't think about the missed kick. In fact, it's usually best not to think too much. Just watch the ball, kick from instinct, and trust your training.

That's what sin is like. It takes decades of practise to "hit the mark". You are just starting. Of course, in the beginning, you're going to be a bad archer. The only way to get better is to keep shooting.

Sin with a Capital S

The Catholic Church teaches that *"mortal sin"* is when you do something morally wrong and it has the following characteristics: Full knowledge, full consent and grievous matter.

I don't know anybody who has full knowledge of the consequences of their actions. I know I don't. I don't know anybody who fully understands what is morally right and what is morally wrong. I know I don't. I don't know anybody who has ever had full consent when they act. I know I don't. All my actions are constrained by my personality, character, history and circumstances. And when it comes to grievous matters. I have no idea what a grievous matter is and what a minor one is. And I certainly don't trust the Catholic Church to tell me. Mortal sins are very, very rare. When Jesus and St. Paul were talking about Sin, they weren't talking about that.

St. Paul and the gospels are not concerned with individual sins, they are concerned with Capital 'S' Sin. This Sin is primarily collective just as the salvation that the Gospels describe is collective salvation. We're all in this together. No one gets saved alone, no one goes to Heaven alone. We are part of one cosmos, one creation. One great story and God is the Author, bringing it all to fulfilment.

When thinking about Sin, and all human activity, the whole is greater than the sum of its parts. If you look at the great trauma of our age, much of it is driven by our over-consumption, ecocide, war, greed and condemnation of others. These are all things that we do collectively. We have a political and economic system that is based on greed and self-interest. And this system is consuming the entire planet. This is Sin.

For me, the best way to understand Sin, is as the opposite of the beatitudes. Remember the beatitudes spelled out by Jesus were the "attitudes of being" that we needed to live fully as sons and daughters of God. That part of us that resists the spirit of the beatitudes is Sin.

Money, pleasure, power and status are not bad things. But that part of us that makes the pursuit of those things the centre of our lives is Sin. It's a dead end and it won't bring joy.

That part of us that that resists the call to hunger and thirst for righteousness, that resists mercy, that does not make God (Love) the centre of our lives. This is Sin. Remember, God is love and wherever love is refused or denied, we find Sin. Whatever takes us away from the love of others, and the natural world, there we find Sin.

Richard Rohr says, "We are not punished *for* our sins, but *by* our sins!" This tendency in us to seek things that are not love, causes us pain, because we are made to live in love.

Learning to overcome this tendency is as difficult as learning to kick a football. But the good news is, even if you're not a very good footballer, you can still play the game. And the more you play, the more you practise, the better you get.

So what does this mean for love? Bubbling away in our hearts and minds is a ferment of pride, desire for power, pleasure and status. Trying to work out what love is calling us to means constantly navigating around the shadows of our own sinfulness. But don't worry. Even if you get it wrong (and you certainly will sometimes), just put your hand up, apologise to your team mates, and get back into the game.

14

Pain, Suffering and God

The Problem of Pain

Have you ever felt great physical pain? Have you ever felt deep sadness that made you weep? Have you ever been rejected and felt unloved? The chances are at some point in your life, you have experienced some if not all of these things. These are all examples of pain. Pain can be defined as an unpleasant sensory or emotional experience.

When we feel extreme pain or feel it for a prolonged period of time, we often call it suffering. When I bump my head, it hurts but the pain soon goes away. When I'm kept awake all night because of a toothache it also hurts but I would usually describe the lingering pain as suffering. This is a common definition of suffering but later in this chapter, I will create a different definition of suffering.

Everybody feels pain and at some point in our lives we all suffer to a greater or lesser extent. But sometimes the suffering in the world seems so great that it forces us to question the very meaning of life itself. When children starve due to a famine, when families are torn apart by war or flood. When we see or experience something so awful that it takes our breath away, we often ask, "How can this be?"

The existence of suffering leads to one of the most powerful arguments against the existence of God and meaning in life. In fact, it's probably the argument that is most persuasive for atheists. I have often heard people say, "How can there be a good God when there is so much suffering in the world?"

The argument against God based on the existence of suffering runs as follows...

If God is all good, She would not wish Her creatures to suffer.

If God is all powerful, then She would be able to achieve Her wish.

But Her creatures suffer, so therefore, God is either: not all powerful, not all good, or not existent.

I am not not convinced by this argument. I still take the leap of faith and give my heart to the idea of meaning and the existence of a loving God. But the existence of suffering and the argument against God's existence based upon it, still confronts me with a profound and seemingly intractable question. *"How can a good, all-powerful God, allow suffering in the universe?"*

In this chapter, I'm going to unpack this question using faith, reason and the mystical way of knowing we discussed in chapters 10, 11 and 12.

We'll begin with reason and follow the the logical progression as far as we can. Reason can't answer all the questions raised by suffering but the process will give us some very important insights in our quest for meaning.

The argument from suffering hangs on three essential elements.
  i) The nature of suffering and pain
  ii) God's power
  iii) God's goodness

Let's work through these three elements in order and then try to apply the insights we gain to our quest for meaning.

Definition of Suffering, Definition of Pain

We often use the words "pain" and "suffering" interchangeably. In the previous section I suggested that some people describe pain as a short-term thing and suffering as a longer, more prolonged discomfort.

Buddhism describes pain as being an essential aspect of life but suffering is something caused by our attitude to the pain. There is real wisdom here but I'm not convinced that the Buddhist definitions of pain and suffering are enough to help us address the questions of meaning raised by the existence of suffering and pain.

We still need to pursue the definitions a bit more. What is the difference between pain and suffering? Here are some examples from my own life that may shed some light on this.

i) As I write this section, the football finals are just around the corner, so football is front and centre in my mind at the moment. I was a terrible footballer. I was the last person picked on my team and my team was pretty poor.

The thing about playing football is, that it hurts. Making a tackle hurts, going into a pack hurts, laying a shepherd hurts like hell, even kicking the ball is mildly uncomfortable if you're not a very good footballer.

But I must tell you, kids, it's been forty years since I've last played a game of football but I still dream about playing it and my football playing dreams are some of my favourites. Playing football is awesome, even though it hurts. Football players endure the pain joyfully as part of the game. There's pain in football, but no suffering.

ii) Going to the dentist sucks. I hate having people interfere with my body and sticking metal instruments in my mouth. And it hurts. I always put off going to the dentist for as long as I can, but eventually, I know that I ought to. So I steel myself and go. It hurts, it's unpleasant, I hate it, but I know it's good for me, so I choose to endure the pain. This is pain but not suffering.

iii) When I had my children, I experienced a kind of love that I'd never had before. It utterly dwarfed the love I had for my parents and my brother and sister. Some of the greatest joys in my life have been just hanging out with my children.

Now my children are adults and have children of their own. They don't have time to hang out with me. Their lives are full and busy, as they should be. But I still yearn for those days when we played board games or read books or told stories.

I know that this yearning in me is painful, but I also know that this pain is an essential part of my love for them. I raised my children to become adults and go out into the world to make their own way, not to remain children. If they were to stay here with me, playing games, reading books, telling stories, it may be pleasant for me, but that would not be loving them. True love must be willing to let go and endure the pain of loss. This is pain but not suffering.

iv) When my daughter, Hannah was a little girl, we lived in an outer island of Fiji for two years. Hannah, being the youngest, was still in primary school. Her school was in the main town about seven kilometres away while the secondary school, where the rest of us were working, was in our village. Every morning I would walk her to the bus to go to school.

She would cry and say, "I don't want to go to school. Let me stay home, Dad."

"I know, darling," I'd reply, "But you have to go."

"Why?" she would wail.

"I can't explain why. I just know you've got to go."

She would cry and plead and whimper all the way down the road and I would listen and make sympathetic noises.

When we'd get to the bus, I'd say, "O.K. Pull yourself together now. Get on the bus and don't let them see that you've been crying."

She'd wipe her eyes miserably and climb aboard.

As the bus pulled away, I would sob and cry all the way to my classroom. Where I would straighten up, wipe my eyes and walk in with a confident smile.

I endured the pain because I knew that going to school was good for her. I wasn't suffering. I was enduring pain. Hannah felt like she was suffering because she couldn't understand why she had to go to school all the way into town when everyone else in the family stayed in our village.

Can you see the pattern here? Pain we have *chosen* is not suffering. Why do we choose pain? The only time anyone chooses pain is when there is a reason for it or a higher reward. It's when we don't chose the pain, when the pain seems to have no purpose, that we suffer. If I haven't chosen it, or I can't see the purpose of it, then I complain and rail against it. When I have chosen it, if I can see a purpose to it, then I can endure it.

So we can define pain as an unpleasant sensory or emotional experience, and we can define suffering as unchosen pain without a higher purpose.

Remember in the first chapter we discussed how the two concepts of meaning and purpose are closely related. It's a very short leap between purposeless pain to meaningless pain.

Pain is intrinsic to human life and not all pain is bad. But when we declare pain meaningless it leads us to question the existence of God and whether life has any meaning at all.

Meaningless Pain as an argument against God

So where does this leave us? Let's rephrase the argument from suffering...

> Suffering is pain without higher purpose
> Something without higher purpose is meaningless.
> Therefore suffering is meaningless pain.
> Suffering is endemic among living things.
> If life has meaning, then every aspect of life must be meaningful.
> Therefore, the existence of meaningless pain proves that life has no meaning.

When expressed this way, it's clear to see the strength of the argument. Let's leave aside the way the argument equates purpose and meaning. That's an expression of how we feel more than a philosophical reality. The main part of the argument hangs on the idea, *"If suffering has no meaning, then life has no meaning."*

Expressed in this way, the argument contains a very important assumption. The argument assumes that if life has meaning, there can't some parts that are meaningful and other parts that are not. Life is either all meaningful or all meaningless. If there is one meaningless aspect to life, then the whole edifice of meaning comes crashing down.

This assumption is not necessarily true. I think it's possible to have a meaningful universe where some parts have meaning and other parts are meaningless and many pagan religions believe this.

Imagine a page of writing where the text means something but there's an ink smudge or a spelling error that has been crossed out. The presence of the smudge doesn't detract from the overall meaning of the text.

But this view of the Universe is not consistent with the teaching of Jesus or the Judeao-Christian Tradition. Most contemporary theists believe that an all powerful, good God has created the whole universe and it is all meaningful. There's no room in the Christian story for a God that makes spelling mistakes and has to cross it out and start again.

As a result, the existence of suffering (meaningless pain) is a powerful argument against the Christian idea of God, but not necessarily an argument against any meaning or any divine author. God (the source of meaning) may still exist but may not be all powerful, or all good.

So Christians are certainly challenged by the existence of suffering but those who claim that life is meaningless are challenged by just about everything else. If life is meaningless, then how is love meaningless? How is childbirth meaningless? How is goodness, mercy, self-sacrifice meaningless?

From an atheist point of view, the metaphor of the text with smudges on it doesn't answer these questions. Even if 90% of the page is covered in meaningless smudges, the 10% that actually means something makes the whole document meaningful. There's still a language, a context, a message embedded in the document that the smudges have not removed. To declare the whole document meaningless, every part of it must be meaningless.

There is another problem with the argument from suffering described at the start of this section. The argument assumes that pain we haven't chosen is meaningless because there was no purpose to it. But the fact that I don't understand the purpose of the pain doesn't make it meaningless. I may think that I'm suffering but the pain may have a purpose I can't see. My pain may fit into a larger frame of meaning that is beyond my understanding.

When I was a child, we used to take our dog to the vet. The vet would give him an injection and the poor dog didn't like it. The dog thought he was suffering. But he wasn't. The vet knew that this was pain with a purpose. It was just that the dog lacked the capacity to understand the purpose of his pain.

We are like two dogs at the vet, debating our situation. One dog (a Theist) is trying to argue that the suffering has a purpose but that purpose is beyond a dog's understanding. The other dog (an Atheist) argues that because neither dog can understand the purpose, then there is no purpose to the suffering.

The two dogs are stuck in an endless argument. Neither dog has the capacity to understand the purpose of their pain. It's simply impossible to prove or disprove anything that is beyond a being's understanding.

It's as if we're at the bank of another creek but we have three options, not just two. We can leap to a bank where life has meaning but there are bits that are not meaningful. This is a traditional pagan position, where God (the source of meaning) is indifferent to humans. This the Universe like a page with smudges and crossed out sections.

Alternatively we can leap to a bank where life is meaningless. Suffering is meaningless and so is love, hope, goodness, trust, beauty and anything else you can think of, because in a meaningless universe everything must be meaningless. This is Albert Camus' position.

Or thirdly, we can leap to the Judeao-Christian bank of the creek where all reality has meaning and therefore suffering must have meaning too.

This leaves those of us who have taken the Christian leaps of faith still wrestling with the problem caused by suffering. *Why does a good, all-powerful God allow us to suffer?* If we are going to address this question, we must consider the nature of God's power next.

Thomas Aquinas and the Power of God

When we say that 'God is all powerful', we usually mean that God can do anything. Surely a perfect creator who created *everything* from nothing must be all powerful. But Thomas Aquinas has argued that there must be some fundamental limitations to God's power and most theologians accept his view.

According to Aquinas, some things are *intrinsically impossible*. In other words, they cannot exist because their existence contradicts themselves.

For example, a square circle can never exist in a two dimensional plane. This is because a circle, by its very nature, cannot be square. This concept is expressed in philosophy by the statement; *A thing can't 'be' and 'not be' at the same time.*

A being cannot exist and not exist at the same time. A thing can't get bigger and not get bigger at the same time. These things are intrinsically impossible.

Aquinas says that when Christians assert that God is all powerful, there's an unspoken exception to the claim. What we mean is that God can do anything that is not intrinsically impossible. Things that are intrinsically impossible are non-things. As C.S. Lewis says, "We can't turn nonsense into sense simply by prefacing the statement with the words 'God can'".

The trouble is, there's no way for us to know with certainty what is intrinsically impossible and what is not. There is a lot we don't understand.

How does intrinsic impossibility affect the problem of suffering? If someone was to put my hand into a fire, it would burn, and my hand would hurt. I'd suffer. The effect of too much heat on my body leads to pain, but how wonderful is the feeling of putting your hands close to the fire on a cold winter's night. Not to burn them, but to warm them.

These two experiences consist of the same interaction between skin and heat. It *may* be intrinsically impossible for a creature to feel the pleasure of warmth without being vulnerable to burning. It may be intrinsically impossible for a corporal being to feel any physical pleasure without being vulnerable to physical pain.

Loneliness and rejection can be sources of terrible suffering. But the joy of companionship, laughter and love is the greatest thing in the world. It may be intrinsically impossible to create a universe where there is love without the possibility of the absence of love.

As we think through examples of pain, we can always find an example of pleasure that seems to be intrinsically bound up with it. It seems likely that some pain is inescapable in a world where there is joy and pleasure.

Now, maybe, God could have created a universe where there was pleasure but no pain. But think for a moment what sort of existence this would be.

Imagine a game of football where the opposition, not only never kicked a goal, but never even got the ball. Every contest, every bounce went our way. How long would you be able to play that game without losing interest?

I suggest that it wouldn't take long. In fact, we'd probably call the game meaningless. What's the point of playing a game that is impossible to lose?

We've now hit another problem. When confronted by defeat, failure and pain, we often declare the game of life to be meaningless. But if the game had no failure, pain or defeat, we'd use exactly the same term to describe it... *meaningless*!

How can we resolve this? For those of us who have taken the leap of faith to declare life meaningful, we must now turn to the question of the goodness of God.

The Goodness of God

We have discussed the limits of God's power and the nature of suffering and in both instances we have run up against the limitations of our own intellect. We don't know what is possible and what is intrinsically impossible. We also can't know with any certainty whether the pain we experience is meaningful or meaningless. However, in this third section of our discussion, we do not come up against such an intractable problem.

Even though the goodness of God is beyond our understanding, and the very existence of God is uncertain, we can understand a lot simply by applying our own heart and intellect to the problem. In his book, "The Problem of Pain", C.S. Lewis addressed this question. In this section, I will summarise his argument.

When Christians talk about the goodness of God, we usually mean that God is just or fair but beneath those concepts is something deeper. We believe that God loves us. When faced with pain that seems to have no purpose, we ask, how can a God who loves us allow us to experience suffering (pain with no meaning or purpose)?

The problem with this question is that it fails to address the nature of God's love. Lewis argues that we often expect God's love to be like the love of a kindly old grandfather. For Lewis, a grandfather takes the attitude that it doesn't matter what a child does, so long as they are happy. They can eat as many lollies as they like or avoid all their chores. The comfort and pleasure of the child comes first.

But God's love is not like that. Lewis uses three analogies to illustrate the nature of God's love for us.

The first is that God's love for us is like the love of an artist for his great work. The artist works on their artwork night and day. Continually trying to improve it, changing bits, removing imperfections and adding new elements, to make it a great masterpiece. Lewis says that if the work of art could think, it may well wish that the artist would leave it alone, but then it would be wishing for less love, not more.

The second analogy Lewis uses is that God's love for us is like an owner's love for her pet dog. The dog would like to be left alone, to wallow in mud and ramble around the fields like a wild dog. But the owner does not leave it alone. She bathes it, she trains it to not chew the furniture, to only poo outside, and as a result she introduces the dog to a much higher form of existence.

The third analogy Lewis uses, is that God's love for us is like a parent's love for their child. The parent doesn't give the child everything they want. The parent insists on the child eating well, being responsible for others and being polite.

When I was raising my children, I was not satisfied with any flaws. I wanted them to be the best they could be. They had to be wise, compassionate, brave and humble. Anything less was not good enough. They would often complain and say, "How come so-and-so is allowed to do this when I am not?" And I would reply, "I don't care about so-and-so. You're my daughter and I love you."

This is the analogy that Jesus used. God is our loving Father. God is not satisfied with us being less than the best we can be. She works on us day and night. Constantly improving us, making us grow, teaching us wisdom and compassion. Because She wants us to grow up and be like Her. As Jesus says, "You must be perfect, like your heavenly Father is perfect." Matt 5:48

In the last section, I described how I would send my daughter Hannah to school. I sent all my children to school, knowing full well that they were going to suffer there. I knew they would get bullied, I knew they would encounter teachers who were not competent, I knew they would be misunderstood and not fit in. But I knew my children had to experience that, if they were to become the best that they could be. They had to learn to cope.

In the same way, it's as if God has sent us into this world, fully aware that we are going to suffer, be rejected, get sick and eventually die, because She knows that we have to experience all of that to become what we are meant to be.

I've often thought that life is like being thrown into a washing machine. We have moments of exhilarating joy, and breathtaking pleasure. And then periods of terrible sadness, trauma and suffering. We are tossed from one extreme to the other and we have no idea why this is happening to us. But God knows. God knows that this is the only way to make us grow up and share fully in the divine life.

Suffering and Transformation

If we believe that life has meaning and that God is good, then we must assert that there is a higher purpose that makes all our pain worthwhile. Jesus said that we are sons and daughters of God and our highest purpose is to grow up to become like God. Therefore everything that happens to us in our lives must contribute to that transformation in some way. In other words, what we call suffering is actually pain that makes us more like God. How can this be?

Richard Rohr says that if there was ever a "Garden of Eden" or spiritual golden age, it would have consisted of people who were loved very well at the centre of their lives and suffered very much around the edges.

According to Rohr, most of the disfunction in the human heart is because we lack a sense of being loved. When a person knows in their deepest heart that they are loved unconditionally, then there is no need to chase wealth, power, status or popularity. Being loved is one of the two great paths to transformation. The other great path, Rohr says, is suffering.

To fully grasp this part of the discussion you'll need to engage your mystical way of knowing. You'll need to find times of silence, where you can sit with these ideas and reflect on them. You'll need to ask yourself, "If this were true, what would this mean for me?" You'll need to let the ideas soak into you and give them time to grow.

In many instances, suffering causes us to be dragged out of our obsession with our own lives. When we are young, we often think that life is all about me. In fact this is not true. *We are about life.*

This realisation that we are not the centre of the universe only occurs to us as a result of suffering. Through suffering, we experience powerlessness and we realise that we cannot control everything. The more we suffer, the more we realise how little we can control, and the wiser we become.

Suffering also opens up spaces within us for compassion. If I have experienced loneliness, then I am more likely to respond compassionately to another person who is alone. If I have been sick, I am more likely to understand the pain of another who is sick. A person who has never suffered, is more likely to be selfish than a person who has suffered. In this way, suffering can connect us to others and make us a more loving person.

Suffering also causes us to reach out beyond ourselves. If I didn't suffer, I could easily end up living a small, self-centred life where I am in control, and there is nothing beyond my own horizon. When I suffer, I am forced to reach out to others for help, and ultimately to reach beyond my small existence in search of meaning. Suffering often leads us to God.

Remember, Christians believe that the Paschal Mystery is the definitive template for the meaning and purpose of life. Right in the middle of it, is the suffering and death of Jesus.

According to Lewis, there is only one way to transformation. Only one way to grow up and share fully in the divine life. That is the way of the cross. The painful and difficult journey through death, into resurrection.

If you're anything like me, you're probably going to recoil from this. Fair enough. In the next section I'm going to try to confront some of the objections to Lewis' argument and see where this leaves us.

Suffering and Trust

This section can be read as a discussion between your rational way of knowing and your mystical way of knowing. Both sides of the argument have merit and you should not discount either of them. Just like there are many ways to love, so there are many ways to know. When I'm inviting you to engage in the mystical way, the words will be in *italics*. You'll need to sit with them, reflect on them, let them soak into your heart rather than your head.

Firstly, you may be thinking, "God sounds like a bit of an arsehole. She inflicts suffering on us to make us reach out to Her. What loving parent would do that!?"

But God is not sitting outside of the world, inflicting suffering *on* us. God is inside the world, sharing in the suffering. Or maybe it's better to say that the world is participating in the suffering of God.

Remember, the Paschal Mystery is not only a metaphor of the meaning and purpose of human life. It is also metaphor for the eternal nature of God.

All reality exists within the body of Christ (Logos). It is God who suffers in Jesus on the cross and says, "I own this. I hold this." Including the most awful cruelty imaginable.

All Love leads to suffering and God is Love. We are children of God and therefore destined, by our very nature to suffer just as She does.

As we grow from undeveloped children to share fully in the divine life of the Trinity, it's inevitable that we love more and therefore suffer more.

Let me try a parable...

> Imagine three bored children playing indoors on a summer day. One child catches a fly, pulls off its wings and says, "Look! I've made a walk."
>
> The youngest child would never dream of pulling the wings off a fly but he finds the joke funny and laughs. The eldest child is horrified. "How would you feel if a giant pulled off your arms?" She scolds. But she is trapped. Does she kill the fly, putting it out of its misery, or put it outside where it can fall victim to predators or leave it alive indoors to be a source of humour for her siblings?

Which of these three children is most loving? Most like God? Which one is suffering? Of course, it's the eldest child. But she's not suffering anywhere near as much as the poor fly, and this reveals another serious problem with this way of looking at suffering.

You're probably thinking, "Come off it, Grandpa.... God puts us into this world because somehow the suffering will all be good for us? Really? What about those people for whom, suffering is not just a brief down period, but part of their daily reality? What about those people who do not grow through their suffering, but are broken by it? The innocent child who is a victim of horrific sexual abuse who then grows up to become an abuser himself or the one who suffers through a life of pain and grief bearing an incurable disease, or the parents of disabled children who are crushed under the weight of their responsibility? Are you seriously telling me that it's all going to be alright in some "happy ever after" heavenly future?

And what about the non-human suffering? The rabbit, screaming as it is taken by the fox? The mouse tortured by a cat honing its hunting skills? The eagle slowly dying of starvation as it fails to find food? Is that all part of the great Paschal Mystery? It may be true that death and resurrection is a pattern in the universe, but it's a long bow to claim that <u>every</u> crucifixion ends in resurrection."

Faced with this argument I have to raise my hands in surrender. I *believe* that the Paschal Mystery is a universal pattern. This is a statement of faith not an argument based on fact or reason. I can point to many examples where death leads to resurrection, but there are also many, many deaths that seem to have no resurrection... yet. In those cases, we find ourselves like Mary Magdalene, weeping at the tomb, waiting for the stone to be rolled away. But we have no idea when or whether the great resurrection will come.

Hans Kung says that every attempt to explain suffering theologically will fail. Ultimately, he says, suffering cannot be explained, it can only be endured, trusting in the love and goodness of God.

When I was teaching, I would leave it there. Often the more words we say, the more rubbish we speak, so it's best to fall silent. But this is a problem that never goes away, you will wrestle with this for the rest of your life. I know I have. And so, even though I may sound like a fool, I will leave you with some ruminations that have grown out of my own mystical way of knowing. Feel free to ignore them or laugh at them, or pray about them.

Consider an apple growing on a tree. Imagine you walk up to that tree, pick the apple and eat it. It goes into your stomach and you absorb the molecules of the apple. The apple becomes part of you. When does the apple become part of you?

When the apple molecules enter the cells of your body?

When the molecules enter your blood stream?

When your gastric juices dissolve the pieces of apple in your stomach?

When you swallow the apple?

When you chew the apple and the enzymes in your saliva start to break it down?

When you bite off a piece of apple and it's in your mouth?

When you pluck the apple from the tree and it's enveloped in your hand?

Or is it when it's hanging from the tree, basking in the afternoon sun?

We have been raised to think of ourselves as individuals. We think there is a clear division between "me" and "not me". We look out at a universe that seems to consist of discrete objects, like billiard balls. A person, a tree, a cloud, a stone, a cow or a star.

But is this perception true or is it illusion? Does the apple have any meaning, apart from the tree? How can we think of a tree as being distinct from the ground in which it grows, or the sun that shines on it, or the rain that waters it?

Even the most rudimentary reflection on nature will show us that we are all part one great system, one living planet utterly dependent on our star. Our concept of individuality is nothing more than an intellectual construct, a metaphor that must not be taken too literally or too seriously.

From a theological point of view, if God is immanent in the universe, and the very essence of existence is the divine Logos, then we are all connected to God and to each other. When you love, the other's joy becomes yours, their suffering becomes your suffering.

God is Love. If Love is the ground and horizon of all being, the essential building block of everything that is, then there is no such thing as 'my suffering' and 'your suffering'. There is no 'your joy' and 'my joy.' We are all part of one creation.

The rabbit screaming in the jaws of the fox, the birds singing joyously in the trees, the couple making love ecstatically by the fire, the man screaming in agony, "My God, My God! Why have you forsaken me!" are all one. One world, one creation.

St. Paul says that all creation groans in one great act of giving birth. The joys, the griefs, the triumphs and defeats are all part of this labour. And God is right in the middle of it, pushing and groaning, giving birth to this new divine life that we are all destined to share.

We are not born alone, we're born into a family, a community, an ecosystem. We don't suffer alone, we suffer as part of the whole of creation. We don't die alone, our death is a small part of the great death that is essential to all living things. So, if the Paschal Mystery reflects reality, then we are not resurrected alone, we are resurrected as part of the new creation.

This reflection doesn't explain or alleviate any of my suffering, but it does give me comfort. It reminds me that I am part of something much much bigger and more complex than my puny intellect can comprehend. And in that awareness, I find it easier to trust.

15

Prayer

Prayer: Listening to the Music

In Chapter 11 we discussed the metaphor of the Trinity. From this metaphor we derived two other metaphors that are trying to express the same reality.

The first was the idea that God is Love and to live a meaningful life we must live immersed in Love. The second was from the early Greek mystics who depicted the Trinity as a Divine dance.

I used this metaphor to represent the whole of creation, as being part of one Divine dance and that we are all invited to join. It is this great dance that provides the context that gives everything meaning. In this metaphor, The Holy Spirit is the music, resonating in our hearts and calling us to get up and dance.

If the Holy Spirit is the music, then before and we can join in the Dance, we have to listen to this music and move to its rhythm.

Putting it another way, if we are to live in Love, we need some way to connect with the ultimate source of Love in our own hearts. That means listening to God, the immanent *Logos* and the still, small voice of the Holy Spirit deep in our hearts. In Christian tradition, this is called Prayer.

There's no right or wrong way to pray, just like there's no right or wrong way to dance. In this chapter, I will discuss the way I pray in the hope that it might help you to develop your own ear for "the divine music."

St. Paul wrote that we should "pray without ceasing" (1Thess. 5:17). If Paul was thinking about prayer as sitting in front of a candle, or meditating on the bible, or kneeling before a statue or saying a Hail Mary, then it's simply not possible to pray without ceasing. To pray without ceasing must mean that we pray all the time. When working, when eating, when reading, talking to friends, having sex etc. Aside from being a bit creepy, it's just not possible. So what did St. Paul mean when he was telling us to pray without ceasing?

The simplest explanation of that text is that Paul defined prayer as *being aware that we are in the presence of God*. In that sense, Paul is arguing that we should always be aware that we are in God's presence. Not that God is an invisible person standing beside us separate from ourselves and the rest of reality, but that our very existence is within God. We are immersed in God, like a sponge in the ocean. God is present to us in and through everything we experience. In every encounter, we encounter God.

Great mystics are profoundly aware of God's presence at all times, but for me, I'm constantly distracted. That's why, the easiest way for me to pray, is by using the simplest form of prayer; talking to God.

There are many people who have a deep and profound prayer life. Great mystics who have written wonderful books and reflections on the art of prayer. I'm not one of those. I told you earlier that I am a terrible mystic. Well, I'm a terrible prayer too.

My prayer life today is not much different to what it was when I was 13 years old. It's very basic, very simple, maybe even simplistic. But I'm okay with that. It works for me.

When I was a young man, I read the great classics on prayer and meditation but they bored me shitless. I've now resigned myself to the fact that I'll never be a Thomas Merton or Theresa of Avila. I'm just daggy Darren Koch.

This chapter could be considered an introduction to prayer. If you want to go deeper, there are plenty of wise people and great works that can guide you. But if you want a simple way to get started, you can try what I do.

When I was a teenager, I used to think that listening to God was very weighty and difficult. After communion at Mass, I used to see my parents and people in church with their heads bowed, deep in prayer. I wished that I too could have that level of devotion, but every time I tried, I found myself thinking about the football or the pretty girl in the pew ahead of me.

In year seven my Maths teacher told us that prayer was simply talking to God. Remember I told you how we used to watch movies in year seven based on Old Testament stories? The Patriarchs all talked to God as if She was standing right beside them. This became the basis of my prayer life, and it still is to this very day. I just talk to God. I talk to Her about whatever's on my mind.

Pretty ladies and the football still make up a lot of my prayer, but sometimes I talk about the garden or the news, or the people I love. It's very, very easy. My daughter Rachael, describes God as my imaginary friend, and to be frank, that's a pretty good description of how I pray. I talk to God as if She's my imaginary friend. The only difference here, is that I actually believe that She exists.

Sometimes I talk to God when I'm driving, or when I'm working in the garden. Sometimes I talk to God when I'm walking through the shops or reading a book.

Often, I forget that God is around and I don't talk to Her at all. I simply get caught up in the minutiae of my daily life.

That can be a problem, because that's when I forget that I am in God, that God is in me and that the whole of creation is a manifestation of God. When I forget this, I may not hear the music and I may lose touch with the dance.

The good news is, that God wants me to hear the music, so as long as I consciously want to hear the music too, God will keep raising the volume until I start dancing. Prayer is basically God's business. It's God's problem. I just have to agree. And I agree in a very half-arsed way.

Prayer: I Talk to God and God Talks to me

Now I must come to a more difficult issue and if you've been sticking with me all the way through, you may be about to cringe and close this book, thinking, "Gee... poor old Grandpa really was a little bit crazy, wasn't he?"

If the band is playing Rock and Roll but we insist on dancing a waltz, we're going to find it hard to keep time with the music. If we want to dance, we have to listen to the music.

Listening to the music is not just me talking. I talk to God, and She talks back to me. I know this may sound strange but seriously, think about it. Why would you pray if God never replied? What's the point? If God wasn't talking back, I would have stopped praying decades ago. But She does talk back, and that is the most important part of the process.

That's why some of the best prayers cultivate silence. When we are silent, and removed from noisy distractions, there is space for God to "speak". Many people pray with their bodies, bowing, sign of cross, yoga postures. These are all ways of creating silence within us to make space for God.

Whatever method of prayer that works for you is fine. There's an old saying, "Pray as you can, not as you can't".

Talking to God is just my way of becoming aware of God's presence and opening the channels of communication so She can talk to me. If you rule out the possibility of God talking to you, then you explain away everything that God does and nothing gets through. You are alone and you can't hear the music.

Fortunately, God can deal with that problem (remember our last chapter - She uses suffering) but that's not what I'm going to talk about here. I want to talk about the active process of prayer.

Letting God talk to you is scary, because you don't know what She's going to say. What if She tells to you to go off to give a message to the meanest, scariest bad guys on the planet, like poor old Jonah in the Bible story (That is a ripping story and is one of the best parables of the life of prayer ever written).

So, if the first step in prayer is talking to God, the second is agreeing to let God talk to you. This requires a willingness to accept whatever God says even if it's something we don't want to hear.

This is best described as an attitude of obedience. It's an openness to God's call, based on trust. We have to trust that God will never ask us to do something that is beyond our capacity. It's like jumping off the table and trusting that She will catch us. And even if She doesn't, we have to trust that She will raise us up if we fall. Yes. It's fucking terrifying!

But it's also really exciting. God, the eternal ground and horizon of all being, is bringing creation into existence and you are not just an irrelevance in the process. You are a crucial (albeit very small) player in the great cosmic drama. Your life isn't meaningless, you are called to help build the Kingdom of God.

Despite this, we still have to deal with our fear. It's best not to engage with God being fearful, with our barriers up. That just gives power to our egos, our desire for control and our need to make ourselves the centre of the universe.

When we reach out to God in Prayer, we have to give up those things. We need to be ready to respond, ready to say yes.

Two Dangers

When it comes to listening to God, there are two dangers that need to be avoided. I've already mentioned the first one. If you assume that God doesn't talk to you, then you wont be able to hear Her.

You may say, hang on a minute, I may not believe that there is a man outside by bedroom window, but if he starts talking to me, I'll hear him. Surely if God speaks, I'll hear Her even if I don't believe She exists or that She speaks to us.

The problem is, when I talk about hearing God, I don't mean literally hearing a voice or a sound. God is transcendent. A transcendent being, by definition, is beyond our understanding, so any encounter with this being must also be utterly beyond us.

Therefore, all our encounters with God must be mediated through finite reality. A sunset, a symbol, a ritual, a set of words, my own heart rate, my imagination. None of these things are supernatural, but these are the things through which we encounter God.

If we rule out God communicating with us, before we even begin, then every encounter with God becomes just a sunset, or a strong emotion. To listen to God, we have to be willing to look beyond the everyday reality of our lives to see the transcendent reality that lurks within (and beyond).

In this sense listening to God can be understood as being truly present to reality. I spend a lot of my life being distracted, thinking about the future, the past or some daydream or other. I am rarely 100% present and fully experiencing my present moment.

I don't know what things will be like for your generation when you read this, but our culture in the 2020's is swamped with trivial distractions and noise pollution. We are allergic to silence and so we miss out on many things. The whisper of autumn crickets. The music of rain on the roof. The wind in the trees. The song of the birds.

Now you may be thinking, "Bloody Hell, Grandpa! We don't even know if God exists and you're proposing that this possibly non-existent God talks to you through everyday events! Sounds like you're living in a fantasy land."

This is where we run up against the other great danger. That is the human capacity for self-delusion. Every human, no matter how intelligent or educated is always in danger of becoming deluded.

We love being right, and once we've decided that something is true, we tend to act in accordance with this perceived truth. The more we act in accordance with this opinion, the more time, wealth, status, and emotional energy we invest in the "truth" we have accepted. It becomes increasingly difficult to go back and admit that our initial opinion was wrong because it makes a mockery of everything we have invested.

There are many examples of this but the best place to see it is in ourselves. Think about something that you have invested a lot of emotional energy in. Say a football team, or a friendship or community group.

I've chosen these examples because you don't necessarily invest in these things for objectively rational reasons. Your friendship group is usually a product of convenience and shared interest. We tend to choose friends that are fun to be around.

They're not necessarily the smartest or the wisest or even the most moral people we know. I remember there were many guys at school who were very decent blokes, but they weren't my friends because I thought they were boring.

Now imagine one of your friends gets involved with some controversy with another group. This used to happen a lot in primary school. Suddenly everyone's picked a side. Once you're in a side, you belong. Everybody agrees with you and you feel safe and valued. Talking to people from the other side makes you feel uncomfortable. Particularly if their arguments make sense.

This will happen to you throughout your life. You will always be drawn to people who share your basic assumptions and often, these assumptions cannot be verified using pure reason.

As I'm writing this the vast majority of Australians are trapped in a profound delusion. Almost all of us assume that western capitalist civilisation will continue indefinitely and we can continue to increase our wealth, power and energy consumption forever. It's madness, but we have been raised with that belief and even though it is becoming increasingly evident that the belief is false, nobody wants to face the truth.

You can see a similar self-delusion in the debates between atheists and theists. Both sides tend to act certain when it's blatantly obvious that the existence of God is anything but certain. But people invest emotional energy in their beliefs. They write books about them, have arguments about them, even persecute others over them. And the more they invest, the less free they are to change their beliefs. People become entrapped.

That's why I made it a point to tell you that you can always jump from one bank of the creek to the other. There are no rules that make it compulsory to believe in God for ever or not believe in God. You are always free to test out the other bank.

Given our capacity for self-delusion, and the fact that every encounter with God is mediated through finite reality, there is a very real danger of going right off the rails when it comes to listening to God.

Navigating between the two great dangers of denying God's communication and self-delusion is what Christians call the art of *discernment*. Discernment is a crucial element of the spiritual life. I don't think there's a hard and fast set of rules about how to discern God's music but in the next chapter I'm going to spell out in general terms the way I do it.

16

Discernment

What is Discernment

In the previous chapter, I described living a meaningful life as dancing to the Music of the Holy Spirit. But before we can dance, we must make sure that we can hear the music clearly.

If we are to live as Children of God and grow up to be like God, then we must listen to The Holy Spirit's voice as She whispers in our hearts. But we can never know whether we are clearly hearing the whisper of God or whether we are deluding ourselves. In our everyday lives there is a lot of noise. This noise consists of our own internal thoughts, the voices of others and our experiences. This noise can often drown out God's Music and make dancing impossible.

God wants us to "dance" and She wants us to "hear the music" but we are trapped between two dangers. The first is denying that the music we hear is from God and the second is deluding ourselves into interpreting Divine Music in the wrong way. Christians call navigating between these two dangers the art of discernment.

Throughout history, many people have committed unspeakable crimes and caused great suffering, believing that they were "doing the will of God". I strongly believe these people were deluding themselves. What can we do to avoid that terrible fate? The whole point of discernment is to stop this from happening to us.

The Catholic Religious tradition has always had an open mind when it comes to divine whispers. In the Catholic tradition, these are called *private revelation* and they are different from the *public revelation* in the person and message of Jesus. Jesus' revelation is for all humanity (in fact all creation) but private revelation is only relevant to those who receive it. So we can't insist that others follow the whispers of God we hear in our prayer life. You can (and should) share your insights with others but you can't insist that they follow them. They must listen to the divine music for themselves.

Also, private relation must always be subservient to public revelation. If you ever feel that God is calling you to do something that is not loving, or something that goes against the teaching of Jesus, then stop! You are probably being deluded.

In this chapter, I'm going to use a few personal examples to try to spell out a few of the steps I take when responding to God to try to avoid self-delusion. But as with all aspects of the quest for meaning, there is very little certainty here. We can never be sure whether we are hearing God clearly and dancing in time to Her music or if we are making up our own whacky noise and dancing to the wrong tune.

Everything is God

Remember in Chapter 3 when I made the argument that God is immanent? If this is the case, then everything we experience in life is an encounter with God. This experience can be compared to characters in a novel, where the whole novel exists within the mind of the author. Every aspect of the character's reality is a manifestation of the author's imagination. In our case, we are the characters and God is the Author. Every aspect of reality is a manifestation of God. So, me sitting here at my desk in my dressing gown while the rain falls outside, is a manifestation of God. Any encounter I have with the world is an encounter with God.

Discernment is the art of interpreting these encounters with God to provide guidance in our lives. The first step of discernment is responding to every experience with the question: "Is that you, God?"

Of course the answer is always "Yes" because if God exists, She must be immanent therefore every encounter is an encounter with God. But this question is the first step in discernment because discernment must begin with us noticing God's presence in every aspect of reality.

Once we are aware of God's immanent presence, the next question is: "What are you trying to tell me in this encounter?" This is when we need to sift through our thoughts and feelings, considering our encounters until we come up with an insight about what God is trying to tell us or have us do.

I'm going to use the word insight, rather than "God tells us", because it's less confronting and probably more accurate but it's also perfectly reasonable to use symbolic language and say "I believe God is telling me to do something."

The third step of discernment is articulating the insight in a clear testable question. For example, "God, are you telling me to do such and such?"

Once you've got to that point, the more challenging aspects of discernment confront us. The minute we ask the question, the reasons for and against the proposed action start bubbling up. And we have to sort out the right course of action between our motivations (which are genuine manifestations of God) and the theological or moral dimensions (which are also manifestations of God).

One simple test is to ask ourselves, "Do I want to do this?" If the answer is "no," then maybe God is the one pushing me.

If the answer is "yes," then we must ask, "am I doing any harm to myself or others by acting on this? Is my action in keeping with the values and principles of Jesus". If not, then it's pretty safe to discount the idea as not being an insight from God.

Throughout this process we need to keep in mind that we are trying to find our way through competing dangers. The first danger is not responding to the "voice of God" while the second danger is self-delusion and going right off the rails.

We can never have any certainty that we are on the right path. Therefore, sitting with the insight and trying to make sense of it, before we act, is an important step we should not skip, in the process of discernment.

St. Ignatious says that we should sit with various possibilities for insights and test them in our hearts. We should then follow the one that feels most life giving. When I was a young man, a wise lady in my local parish summed up the dilemma of discernment with the phrase, "Do what gives you peace in your heart" but I often found this to be a difficult thing to do.

In all this, it's important to remember that the Holy Spirit rests at the deepest part of ourselves. We are never on our own when it comes to discernment. There is always a part of us in synch with the good, the beautiful and the true. We have our own inner homing instinct and often it's best to simply trust it.

Low Risk and Urgent Insights

Sometimes acting on our insights is low cost and low risk. Say for example, I think God might want me to visit my friend Betty. Betty is lonely, I'm not doing anything this afternoon. It's no skin off my nose to pop over and have a cuppa with her. I have no idea whether I'm acting on divine urging or not, but it's no big deal.

But sometimes, the insight is high cost or high risk. I may feel the need to change the direction of my life or do something that may cost me status or wealth or power. Then I need to tread more carefully.

Most of the time the insights we develop can be considered provisional. What I think God may be saying, may actually be what God is saying or it may not be. I can think about it some more and refine my ideas later because there is no rush or time limit. However, sometimes an insight might be urgent. I might be called to take action quickly, and by acting too quickly, I can run the risk of acting on a delusion.

Years ago, when I was teaching, one of the vice principals of our school moved on to a different school. Another vice principal was giving the farewell speech. He discussed the staff member very briefly and then simply threw the topic out to the rest of us to contribute something.

There was silence. Clearly, no one had been asked to prepare a speech to farewell a man who had devoted two decades of his life to our school. I was appalled. The silence stretched on.

Then I felt that tell-tale burning in my heart, I got the sinking feeling that God wanted me to say something. There was no time to mull over this. I needed to make a snap decision.

The arguments for and against were very clear. It was clear that nobody had anything to say. If I stayed silent, this good and decent man would be sent away from our school without one word of thanks from the teachers. But I had absolutely nothing to say. I liked the guy but I didn't really have a lot to do with him. If I stood up and spoke, I would probably end up making a colossal dick of myself.

I had no time to carefully weigh up the competing motivations of my heart. I had to to either act straight away or not act at all. I had to take a risk. I had to get up and throw myself off the table.

There's a line in the Bible where Jesus says, if ever you're called on to speak, not to worry, the Holy Spirit will give you the words you need at the time. I also knew some of Martin Luther King's best speeches were made when he went off script and "just let the spirit flow".

I stood up and shot a silent prayer heavenward "Shit, Lord! You'd better show up!" And with that, I began to speak, letting the words fall out of my mouth as I thought of them.

I don't remember much of what I said. I know I started off badly. Talking about how when I first came to school, I would watch the man walking urgently across the quadrangle and I thought, "He looks important. I'd like to be like him one day". It got a laugh but it's a terrible opening to a speech. (For future reference, speeches are *not* meant to be about yourself, but about the person you are toasting). I don't remember much else, but I remember talking about his many outstanding qualities and then finished with, "I won't be able to watch him walking across the quadrangle anymore, but I still hope to be like him one day."

Even as I sat down, I knew that it was one of the best speeches I'd ever given. I saw people's eyes filled with tears and the vice principal smiled at me with gratitude. Afterwards people kept coming up to me and saying how good the speech was and how I must have been preparing for quite a while. His wife was deeply moved, taking both my hands in hers and saying with breaking voice, "Thank you so much!" I felt a bit ashamed. Of course, I had not written the speech, but I couldn't give the credit where it was due because people would have thought I was crazy.

In that instance, it seems that it all worked out. No harm was done and a good man was given the farewell speech he deserved. But even now over a decade later, I still can't be sure whether I was following an insight from God or just doing my own thing. I think I was meant to stand up and the Holy Spirit gave that speech, but I will never know. This is an essential part of discernment. We can never be sure.

In this case, the insight was urgent, the risk was moderate and the possible payoff was high. But there are other times when the risk is very high and getting it wrong could causes serious, long-term damage. I'll talk about that in the next section.

When the Stakes are High

Giving your heart to the teachings of Jesus, making love your central motivation and trying to live your life in step with The Holy Spirit's music can be scary but it is also the doorway to a wonderful life of meaning and purpose. Your life is no longer just about you. You become part of a great cosmic unfolding, a new world based on love, peace and justice. And everything you do, no matter how insignificant, plays a small but crucial role in the great plan of God.

I'm writing the first draft of this book now and I don't even know if this paragraph will get into the second draft, let alone survive to publication. But this paragraph matters. This paragraph, which maybe only one or two people will read, will help bring about God's grand plan of Love, because everything is used to bring about God's purpose. No matter how small. Once you've given your heart to the Gospel, nothing you do is insignificant or meaningless. Even the smallest thing matters.

But sometimes we can feel called to do something significant. You may feel that God is calling you to change direction in your life, or take a large risk. The stakes may seem very high to you and risk of failure may seem great. You may be called to leap off a higher table and therefore the risk of falling may seem greater. This call also begins in prayer and requires discernment but the issue may involve more people and may possibly lead to greater suffering for both you and those around you.

The first steps are the same, pray about it, reflect on whether it fits in with the greater values and principles of Jesus, sort out your various internal motives and favour love and courage over fear and comfort.

But in the bigger issues, when you have time to make a considered decision, consulting with others is the most important step. You need to run your ideas past people who you trust and preferably a variety of people. It's always good to get the view of a brother or sister who has also thrown their lot in with Jesus and His message, you can ask them to pray about it as well as you. But it's just as important to run your insight past trusted people who have taken a different leap of faith.

Remember the main thing we are trying to avoid is self-delusion. Religion is a bubbling cauldron of self-delusion. So if at all possible, make sure you get a point of view that doesn't share your religious assumptions as well.

Of course, don't go and check your plans with the president of the local Nazi party. Choose someone whose values you trust. Someone who is compassionate, intelligent and flexible in their thinking. Eventually, as you struggle to sort out the internal and external voices, you will find your way to what God is calling you to.

The best way for me to explain this process may be through an example. Here is an example that has had a huge impact on my life (for good or ill, we don't yet know).

Twelve Steps of Discernment: An Example

1: Every aspect of reality is a manifestation of God.

The summer of 2019/20 was known in Australia as the Black Summer. Starting in the north, in late spring, bushfires raged across our land. By Christmas, the fires had reached Victoria and a thick pall of smoke had settled over Melbourne. The sun rose angry and red every day and the smoke choked our lungs and stung our eyes.

2. The insight emanates out of prayer.

I was sitting on my back verandah with my cup of tea, watching the sunrise and talking to God when I got the distinct impression that these fires were a harbinger of a greater catastrophe. I felt the presence of a looming environmental disaster striking into my heart with full force.

It made me feel like I was in Germany in 1933. Similar to the Jews of that time, there was no altering the trajectory. The only hope was to run.

If I am honest, I'd must admit, that as soon as I felt it, I strongly suspected that it was God, because I felt the tell-tale burning in my heart.

But where would I run too? The Jews who fled Hitler's Germany by going to Poland only delayed the inevitable. In our looming environmental catastrophe, there is no Switzerland. No safe haven. I finished my cup of tea and pushed the insight aside. It was ludicrous.

3. The insight doesn't go away when you try to ignore it.

But like the pall of smoke and raging bushfires of that summer, the feeling didn't fade. It kept nagging at me.

4. Share your insight with others.

I eventually decided to start talking about it to the people I loved and trusted the most. I was very frightened to do this, because I knew what I was saying sounded crazy. But this issue was too serious. I couldn't discern the worth of my insight on my own. I needed other view points.

My insight was almost universally rejected. Yes, things were bad, but there's no need to panic, and there's no guarantee that anywhere else would be better than Melbourne.

My daughters had been involved in campaigning on environmental issues for many years and knew that the system wasn't showing any signs of changing. But they were busy working on the solution and they saw running away as giving up. They also didn't have much sympathy for messages from God (Dad's imaginary friend).

Jen (J'Ma) was incredulous. She had a reasonable understanding of the science but she had not followed it deeply and she certainly didn't want to leave her home. Even my closest Christian confidents were not moved by my insight. They were not getting the same message. In spite of the nagging doubt in my heart, I resolved to stay and fight it out here.

5. The insight bubbles up again.

Later that Summer, my daughter, Rachael and her husband, Matt took a weekend off from their farm and went to the city for a break. It was about 9.30 at night when the phone call came. Rachael had been looking at the most recent scientific research. Neither of us had bothered doing that for over 10 years.

The ten-year-old data showed that things were going to get bad but not until the end of the century, but the most recent data showed that things were happening much, much faster. Rachael, with no reference to God or prayer had arrived at exactly the same insight that I had received on my back verandah. She had to get out to ensure that her children had a chance to live a good life.

Rachael sent me some links to academic papers and so began a long torturous journey into the belly of our collapsing civilisation. The more I looked, the worse the news got, and the call to flee got stronger.

6. We all start sharing the insight with others.

Rachael's research carried much more weight with the rest of the family than my whispers from God. They all started doing some reading and then they started talking to others. But the rest of my family got the same response as I did. No one else would listen. Some people thought we were overreacting, most denied the threat, saying it either wasn't so serious or urgent.

7. Continually being aware of the danger of delusion.

I asked several people, whose scientific expertise and spiritual acumen I trusted to "check my work" to make sure I wasn't deluding myself and panicking over nothing but nobody would. It was too scary, too distressing. With only me and Rachael doing the main research, I feared that maybe everyone else was right, and maybe we were over reacting. "Are we crazy?" Was a constant question we asked each other during those autumn months.

8. Back to Prayer

That was the question on my lips as I sat on my back verandah sipping my tea one Friday morning. "This is nuts, God." I said. "Are you seriously telling us to leave everything behind and start again somewhere else? I'll do it if you want, but I need to know this is what you want. Maybe I should just stay here and live out my days in peace. I'm gonna need some kind of a sign."

9. *Every aspect of reality is a manifestation of God.*

As soon as those words formed in my mind, a huge flock of parrots erupted from the behind the Hub shopping centre and flew across Cranbourne Road and over my house. There were many small parrots around my house in Frankston, but in all the years I had sat on the back verandah, they had never flown directly over my house. They always flew to my left. The timing was uncanny. It definitely seemed like this was the sign I had asked for. I sat, stupefied for a moment, then, "What the fuck does that mean!?"

I don't usually ask God for signs. It's dodgy theology and it all comes down to interpretation anyway. But this was clearly the most shitty sign God had ever given anyone. I skulked off inside complaining and muttering.

10. *Gaining insight from others.*

That weekend, Jen came over as usual and we were watching an episode of one of our T.V. shows. At the end of the episode, as the main characters were moving on to their next adventure, a large flock of birds erupted from the bush behind them and flew directly over the camera. It was uncannily similar to my experience on the back verandah. I was shocked.

"Ooh deep!" said Jen, laughing.

"Um... yeah." I tried to keep my voice light, "But what does it mean?"

She didn't miss a beat. "It means, escape. They got away."
I didn't say anything. Just sat staring at the screen while the credits ran, my heart racing.

11. *Back to Prayer*

On Monday morning I was sitting on my back verandah again, complaining to God. "Jen may think birds flying over her means escape but I'm not buying it. It's all just nuts. That's a shit sign. Are you seriously telling me that a bunch of birds flying over my house means I have to leave?"

And right on cue, as soon as the words were formed, a large flock of parrots erupted from the behind the shopping centre and flew directly over my house.

I lived in that house for another two years and I had a cup of tea on that back verandah most mornings, but I never again saw the birds fly over my house in that way again.

I hope you can see the pattern here. There is a constant dynamic between prayer, experience, reflection, reason and consultation. At every step of the way the process of discernment demands that we be open minded. Open to the possibility of God "speaking" to us, but also constantly aware of the dangers of self-delusion.

12. *There is never any certainty.*

And so, we push on. I am still not at all sure whether this is what God is calling us to do, but I'm acting as if it is. Our family have absolutely no guarantee that we are moving to safety, but we had to chose. We had to decide to either ignore the insight or follow it. And we chose to follow it.

When you're reading this, you may have a better idea than me about whether my discernment was right or wrong. Certainly most of my generation, think I'm a little crazy about this issue, and they may well be right. But I purposely chose this example because I want you to understand two important things.

The first is that one person's insight is not necessarily binding on everybody else, and the second that discernment is never certain. Even years after the fact, we never really know if our discernment is true or delusional.

Secondly, discernment is not about always getting it right but about the honest struggle to do the right thing. The fact is, our heads get things wrong all the time and our hearts and emotions are not far behind. But even when we get it wrong, it's not the end of the world. As the old the Spanish proverb says, "God writes straight with crooked lines."

All we can do is weigh up the issues, choose love and courage over fear and comfort. And then jump off that table.

17

Death and Beyond

Death

I started this book with Albert Camus' claim that death makes everything meaningless. If we are to find meaning in life, we must come up with a world view that is not made meaningless by death.

If we are to assert that life has meaning, then death must also have meaning. This is inescapable. Death is deeply embedded in reality and nothing lives unless something else dies. From the moment you first ate solid food, you lived because something else died. A plant, a fruit, an animal. They died so you could live. Therefore, any meaning in life must include death.

In the Christian religious tradition, there are three elements that need to be central to our quest for meaning. Firstly, Jesus said we are children of God therefore destined to grow up to become like God. Secondly, the Trinity metaphor depicts the fundamental nature of God and reality. And finally, the Paschal

Mystery metaphor depicts the nature of human life, and the shape of the journey we must take to reach that end.

How can we interpret these three metaphors in a way that sheds light on the question of death and the possibility of life after death.

The Paschal Mystery (the suffering, death and resurrection of Jesus) puts death at the very centre of the process. The death depicted here is not some clean, sanitised version of drifting off peacefully to sleep. Death is terrible. We cry out, scream, weep and bleed. We go through it alone and it entails great suffering, physical, emotional and spiritual. There is no easy way to die.

Thomas Merton said that when we die almost everything we think we are is stripped away. This sounds pretty bloody terrifying and it raises a serious question about resurrection. If everything is stripped away and lost, then what is left to be resurrected?

The key insight here is the implied caveat in Merton's statement. He doesn't say that everything we are is stripped away. He says, *almost* everything *we think* we are is stripped away. It's in the "almost" and "we think" where we can find a crack that enables resurrection to sneak through.

Firstly, not everything we think about ourselves is truly who we are. Our self-image is full of illusion and delusion. I used to think of myself "a strong family man," but I was deluding myself. After my daughter's slow death, I found that I wasn't as strong as I thought I was. Letting go of that false self-image was exceptionally painful (it still hurts) but it was a necessary part of my growth.

You have to know who you are before you can live the divine life. Learning who I really am is a kind of dying. My old self-image dies and a new more truthful one takes its place.

Richard Rohr describes this as letting go of our *false selves* and embracing who we truly are. Our false self is a set of agreements between us and our parents, our family, our school friends, our culture and our religion.

It's our launching pad: our looks, our intelligence, our sporting ability and so on. These are the trappings of ego that help us get through an ordinary day.

Our false self is a necessary start, but it can't substitute for the real thing. As we grow, our various false selves have to die as we learn more about our true self.

As our life goes on and our false self-image is slowly stripped away piece by piece, it really feels like dying. But this 'dying' leaves us with our true self, the one who has been invited to the divine dance.

The teenager who was invited to dance with his mother in chapter 11 had a lot of dying to do before he could finally step out onto the dance floor. But he didn't know how much of his self-image was false. He had to let go of his desire to be seen as 'cool' and his fear of making mistakes. He had to have suffered humiliation and rejection so that he can learn that the opinions of others can't destroy him. He simply hadn't died enough to dance with his Mum.

After 63 years of life, some of my false self has been stripped away, but not all. I still have a lot of dying to do. It will be painful and I'm scared of it. But you can't be resurrected unless you die, you can't find your true self unless your false self is torn away. The tearing away of our false selves is excruciating, but there is no other way.

"But Grandpa," you may say. "Finding out that I'm not as smart as I thought I was, or not as pretty as my Dad says I am, is not the same thing as dying."

And you'd be right. Losing our illusions is painful and it feels a bit like dying, but it's not dying. I suspect that dying is much worse. After a failure, or after we are brought down to earth with a hard thud, at least there's still a "me" left to complain about it, to learn from it. But dying seems to be so final. There seems to be nothing left, just a yawning emptiness where there was once a living, laughing, loving presence. Yeah, death sucks! But according to the Paschal Mystery, it's the only way to resurrection.

Life After Death

The ultimate end and purpose of life is resurrection so we can share fully in the divine life but there can be no resurrection without death.

Karl Rahner, a great German theologian of the 20th century says that most people think about death, and life after death in a very simplistic way. He describes this common understanding in the following metaphor.

> *We are riding a horse along a path, until we get to the great river of death. Once we cross over, there we find another horse and we just ride on again exactly the same as before.*

Rahner says this is not consistent with Christian theology.

Every gospel account of the encounters with the resurrected Jesus, show the resurrected body as being different to his original one. Often the disciples don't recognise him at first, he appears suddenly as if the laws of physics no longer apply to him, yet, he eats and can be physically touched. These depictions seem completely contradictory and if you took them literally, you could be forgiven if you thought they were all just bullshit.

But these stories are not to be taken literally. They are attempts to express in symbolic language the apophatic encounters the disciples had with the resurrected Jesus. We must take them seriously, but not literally.

It would seem that the gospel writers are trying to depict a post resurrection reality that is completely different from our understanding. Through the resurrection, the human known as Jesus of Nazareth was completely caught up into the transcendent life of God. No story, image or description can accurately portray that reality. Ultimately, we must fall silent in any attempt to understand life after death. Like God, the divine life that we are raised to, is completely beyond our understanding.

Maybe the best description of death is by Hans Kung, "We do not die into nothingness. We die into God." Everything else is just speculation.

If you read the Bible, searching for clues about life after death, you'll come away with more questions than answers. One of the reasons for this is that there are two competing images that were held by the New Testament authors and The Old Testament adds two more.

The earliest Old Testament writings described death as to "sleep with our fathers". There was no definite statement but it seemed there was not much belief in life beyond death. Later, the Hebrew understanding of death became a shadowy place called *Sheol*. Shadowy not because it was dark and unpleasant, but because we didn't know what lay beyond. There was a hint that the eternal, transcendent God who loves us, would not abandon us in death. But only a hint.

By the time of Jesus, the Jews had developed the idea of a resurrection. According to this belief, at some point in the distant future, God would raise the righteous dead to live eternally. We can see elements of this understanding in many of Jesus' parables.

The other idea in the New Testament grows out of Greek philosophy. Plato thought the human soul was eternal by its very nature and that even though our bodies died, our soul would live on. Many early Christians adopted this idea to imagine that after death, our souls "go to Heaven" where we live eternally with God.

These ideas may have some merit, but we can't take them too seriously. We simply cannot know. And if we did know, we wouldn't have words to describe it.

But the Trinity metaphor gives us some things that we can say about life after death. Firstly, after death, we are still in relationship. God is a relationship. And we already participate in it. The nature of the participation may change but the relationship will not. We will still be loved and still be able to love others.

Secondly, we will not be detached from the natural world. God is not detached from the world. The *Logos* is expressed in and through the cosmos. If we share in the divine life of God, then we will probably also be in some way immanent in the world.

Finally, whatever the divine life is, it's not static. The Trinity metaphor, depicts it as a dynamic relationship that encompasses all of reality. This dynamism must also be a factor in whatever we experience beyond death.

These three elements pop up regularly in the metaphors and parables of Jesus. A banquet, a wedding, a harvest. These metaphors are earthy, communal, celebratory, dynamic.

In the Catholic religious tradition, we have two doctrines (metaphors) that are very popular and reflect the Trinitarian engagement with the world. These are the doctrine of the communion of saints and the doctrine of purgatory. We have a tradition where we pray for the dead (the holy souls in purgatory) and where the dead pray for us (the communion of saints). This is theology way above my pay grade, but there is a common theme here. Our loved ones who die are present to us in God.

I've met many people who describe feeling the presence of their dead loved ones. They are convinced that their loved ones really are with them. Sometimes, I feel that too, but I must confess, I can never really trust that feeling. It could just be my imagination and I'm just not that much of a believer.

Still, I act like I believe it. With Kung, I say we die into God. We enter the divine dance of the Trinity and therefore our dead are as close to us as God is.

> When my Mum was facing her death, she said, "I'm ready to die, but I'm going to really miss you."
> I said with a confidence I didn't feel, "You won't miss me, Mum. You'll be with God in my heart. We'll be together all the time. You'll be sick of me."
> We laughed.
> Then she became serious again and said, "Will you talk to me? When I'm gone."
> I held her hand. "I'll talk to you every day, Mum."
> She smiled, satisfied.

And so I talk to my mum every day. I don't know if she can hear me, but I promised her I would and so I do. I talk to all of my dead loved ones. Mostly words of gratitude, but sometimes words of grief. I assume that they are with me, sharing the divine life. The great Trinitarian dance that I don't understand, but I still choose to believe in.

I want to finish this section with a metaphor that helps me as I face death. We exist in a universe created by God out of nothing. So God must have used Her own self to create everything that is.

A few years ago, I wrote a novel. I created the characters, the setting and the whole world where the novel took place. The book is now finished and sitting on my bookshelf. The characters that I created, existed only in my mind. Their entire lives played out in my internal world. Even though some of those characters died within the novel, they aren't dead to me. They are still hunting, laughing and loving each other within me. For as long as I live, those characters will be alive in me.

When you read this, I will be alive too. I'll be existing in God, just like I am now.

We are characters in God's novel. Our entire existence is within God. Whether we are alive or dead, we are always inside God. My death will be just the end of my part in the story but our existence in God, is eternal because God is eternal.

Heaven and Hell

When I used to teach Life after Death to year eights, the kids used to get quite impatient with my theological ramblings. They wanted to know about Heaven and Hell. Either to dismiss the ideas or to be titillated by them. I was the same when I was teenager, and I don't expect you to be much different.

Christian tradition has spent a lot of time discussing the ideas of Heaven and Hell. We have images of people sitting on clouds, playing harps, whilst down below the Devil and those who are damned are burning in a lake of fire. There are jokes told about Hell where beer kegs have holes in them and beautiful naked women do not. There are images of St. Peter at the gates of Heaven, making sure that nobody unworthy gets in. Most of the jokes are quite funny, and we'd spend at least a lesson telling jokes about Heaven and Hell in my Year 8 R.E. class.

But eventually, we have to face the fact that the jokes aren't real and the traditional images of Heaven and Hell are metaphors that *sometimes* can be taken seriously but never taken literally.

Many of the traditional images of Heaven tell us more about the humans who came up with them than the afterlife. Often people portray Heaven as a place where all sorts of pleasure, wealth and status is available. But Jesus made it quite clear in the beatitudes that pleasure, power, wealth and status, do not give us lasting joy so those things are not going to be the most important part of Heaven.

As I said in the previous section, the images Jesus used to describe life after death emphasised community, celebration and love. The metaphors Jesus used to describe Hell was often, a place of burning or great thirst. Many people therefore assume, that Hell must be a place of physical suffering. Sometimes it can be quite challenging to untangle all the weird and wonderful imaginings of others from the central message of Jesus.

Firstly, neither Heaven nor Hell is a place. There are no gates or fiery furnaces. These are all metaphors. Both Heaven and Hell are states of being.

Heaven is the state of loving and being loved. Heaven is sharing the divine life, engaging fully in the divine dance. It's not a place. It's a way of being. You can live in Heaven, right now, but most of us don't.

Heaven is not an "either/or" reality. There are no gates. The more we love, the more heavenly our life becomes. The more we are true to our deepest nature, the more we are able to appreciate being loved. We don't "get into Heaven", we *grow* into it. As we learn to cast off more of our false selves and embrace love, we live a more heavenly life.

By the same token, Hell is not a place. Hell is the state of not loving. A life without love is agony. It's like burning. We were made to love and be loved. If we are not living in love, then we are living in Hell.

Similarly, Hell is not an either/or reality either. The more you devote your life to power, pleasure, status and money, the more thirsty you will be. You will never be satisfied. The less you love, the more you will live in Hell.

Illusion is one of our greatest enemies. We often think that people who have lots of money or power or status are happy. They are not. It's those who love and are loved who are the happiest in the world.

Hell traps you. The more we strive for power or pleasure or money and status, the more we want. Some people live their whole lives chasing these illusions and their lives are miserable. But they think that they are miserable because they don't have enough money or power or status. They are trapped in Hell. We are not "sent to Hell", we shrink into it.

"But Grandpa," you say, "the Bible talks about God sending people to Hell, separating the sheep from the goats and stuff like that. How can a loving God send Her children to Hell?"

God does not send us to Hell. Hell is a possibility. Ultimately God is responsible for the state of Hell, because She created the Universe the way it is. She gave us free will to choose to live our lives in any way we like. If we choose a life without love, we choose a life of misery. Hell.

Some people imagine that Hell is teeming with people suffering for their sins. Not me. I don't think there are many people in Hell at all. In fact, I wouldn't be a bit surprised if Hell was completely empty.

When my students would discuss the question of being sent to Hell, I would tell them a story. It's not 100% accurate. I've cobbled together a few anecdotes from my life to make my story work. Here is it...

> One Saturday when I was in primary school, my brother and my Dad wanted to watch the cricket on T.V. I thought cricket was boring. I wanted to watch the cartoons.
>
> We argued about it and then Mum said, "It's two against one. Two people want to watch the Cricket and you are the only one who wants to watch cartoons."

I cracked it. I stormed off to my room, slammed the door and sat miserably on my bed, cursing my brother, my father and my Mum.

After a while, Dad knocked on the door to tell me that lunch was ready.

I told him I wasn't hungry and I stayed sulking in my room.

Outside, I could hear conversations and the smell of bacon cooking. The laughter and life of my family went on without me and that just made me even more miserable.

But no one had sent me to my room. No one had condemned me or declared me unworthy. I sent myself. I chose to dwell on the fact that I hadn't got my own way, and as a result, I shut myself off from all the good things that were available to me.

I was in Hell.

There was no way for anyone in my family to rescue me from my Hell, unless I consented. My Father could have physically grabbed me and dragged me to the kitchen table. But I'd still be in be Hell. I'd still be consumed by my grievance and my misery. I was the only one who could free myself.

As you go through your life, be careful not to dwell on past hurts, or nurse grievances. Let them go and keep yourself open to love, loving and being loved. Then you will lead a Heavenly life and when you die, your Heavenly life will continue in God just as it always has.

Conclusion: The Signs of The Times

When I was a teenager in the 1970's, we lived under the shadow of nuclear war, but the danger seemed distant and manageable. By and large my entire generation believed that things would continue to get better, just as they had for our parents. Humanity would continue to increase our life expectancy, our material possessions and our access to energy.

Even your parents had a pretty optimistic attitude when they were teenagers in the early 21st century. They knew that Western civilisation was facing serious problems, but most of their generation felt confident that they could face those problems and overcome them. One of the slogans that did the rounds in those days was "we will be the first generation to eradicate world hunger".

I'm writing this for you in 2025, and the young people of today have no such optimism. There is no great movement calling hopefully for change, just a shared whisper, "Things are not good". They see the climate changing, the nations of the world threatening and fighting, and they see cracks forming in the economy. They are beginning to suspect that owning a home and living a comfortable suburban life will be forever beyond them. Many no longer believe that their lives will get better.

Those who are in power, the politicians, the captains of industry, and the leading scientists, economists, and media outlets, continue to pretend that nothing is wrong. The conservatives claim that we are heading in the right direction, the left claim that we only need to make a few changes and all will be well. In spite of this, people today are beginning to feel in their bones that things will not be well.

By the time you are reading this, my darlings, the cracks will probably be wide and many will be falling through them. The climate breakdown will be undeniable and you will probably be amazed that anyone ever thought that we could have *more* wealth, *more* energy, and *more* control over the world. You may well look back on us as arrogant, entitled, selfish and greedy. And fair enough, we burned your inheritance. I'm sorry. I'm so very sorry.

There were millions of us who tried to change society's direction, but the system was too strong, the powerful were too powerful, the greedy were too greedy and the stupid were just too stupid.

The truth of the matter is, industrial civilisation is dying and it is taking billions of living creatures (both human and non-human) with it. And you must live through the years of its death. We must all find meaning in this era of decline and fall.

There is grief here, terrible grief. There is sadness and fear and anger. And banging on the door, demanding to be let in, is despair. Despair insists that we abandon hope and plunge into a kind miserable nihilism. But I will keep that door firmly locked. I will not give in to despair and neither should you.

If life has meaning, then death has meaning too. If the universe has been called into existence by Love, then every aspect of that universe is part of the great cosmic dance answering only to Love. Our hope is not in human agency or wishful thinking. Our hope is grounded in the Love that holds all creation in Her hands.

As a civilisation, we are experiencing first-hand the Paschal Mystery. We are in *Gethsemane* now. The torches, red on sweaty faces are approaching. Most of our companions are asleep, but Jesus has asked us to stay awake and watch with Him. It's the least we can do. Don't turn away. Don't pretend it's not happening, don't deny reality. *"Watch with me."*

I'm don't know where in the story you will be when you read this, my darlings, but we know how the story plays out. The mocking, the scourging, the suffering, the dying. There is no escape. This is the lot of every individual, every family, every society and every civilisation.

But there can be no resurrection without the cross. There's no way to get from Holy Thursday to Easter Sunday without passing through the horror of Good Friday. Before we can be raised from the dead, we have to die. And there is no easy way to die.

I have had many little deaths and many wonderful resurrections in my 63 years of life. But every little death seemed like *the end of the world* to me at the time. But they were not. They were just relationship break-ups or the death of some plan or ambition. These little deaths were painful but they were not the end of the world. When I close my eyes for the last time and drag in my final, shuddering breath, the world, for me, will end. But the world will not end. It will only end for me.

Civilisations are the same. The collapse of industrial civilisation is not the end of the world. There can still be community, order, peace, security, without this pulsating industrial monster that we are addicted to. There will still be love, family, friendship, music, sex, stories, laughter, joy. All the things that make life worth living are not affected by the collapse of industrial civilisation in the slightest.

But what if our *Via Dolorosa* leads us to extinction? If humans disappear as a species from the earth, that would be very, very sad, but it would not be the end of the world. There will still be birds, rabbits, cats, mice etc. And these animals will continue the great symphony of life.

And even if we plunge the planet into a mass extinction event, leaving nothing but a republic of grass and cockroaches, life will bounce back, and the great symphony will continue, with new species and new ecosystems.

And of course, we know, that our beautiful sun that provides us with all our energy, will eventually expand and scour all life from the earth. We know that one day (scientists think it will be in about 800 million years) earth will become uninhabitable. Even so, I will still hope for one more great resurrection.

The divine dance is eternal.

Glory be to The Father,
And to The Son,
And to The Holy Spirit,
As it was in the beginning,
Is now and ever shall be,
world without end.
Amen

Let it be so.

Select Bibliography

I have not included references in this book but here is a list of the books that have influenced me the most in my quest for meaning.

These books make a good list of what you may want to read next if you are interested.

I've broken the books up into groups based on the type of work and I've written a short comment after each book so you have some idea what you are letting yourself in for if you choose to read them.

Some are easier to read than others so the asterisks are a guide to help you choose books that are suited to your level of literacy and education.

One asterisk * Easiest to read. Senior High School literary level.
Two asterisks * * If you've read my book, you can understand this.
Three asterisks * * * University level literacy required.
Four asterisks * * * * A heavily academic book. Hardest to read.

Fiction, Biography and Poetry
Mitch Albom, 2003, *The Five People You Meet in Heaven* (Novel) *
A metaphor about an old man who dies and goes to Heaven. There he meets five people who explain the significance of his life.

Albert Camus, 1947, *The Plague* (Novel) * *
The French colonial city of Oran is struck by Bubonic Plague and is quarantined. In the book, the plague is a metaphor for death and Camus uses the novel to address the absurdity of the human condition.

T.S. Elliot, 1922, The Waste Land (Poem) * * *
This long poem stares boldly into the abyss of a society that defines meaning only in terms of wealth power, pleasure and status.

Andrew Greeley, 1986, *God Game* (Novel) *
A Catholic Priest accidentally becomes the God of an fantasy, medieval world when lightning strikes as he's playing a computer game.

C.S. Lewis, 1961, *A Grief Observed* (Autobiography) *
After the death of his wife, Lewis kept a journal in which he struggled with grief and his Christian faith. No easy answers here, just grief, and faith.

C.S. Lewis, 1955, *Surprised by Joy* (Autobiography) * *
Describes how Lewis moved from his childhood Christianity to Atheism and then back to Christianity when he was a University Academic in 1931.

Yann Martel, 2001, *Life of Pi* (Novel) *
A shipwrecked teenage boy sails a small lifeboat across the Pacific ocean with a wild tiger on board.

J.R.R. Tolkien, 1954-1955, *The Lord of The Rings* (Novel) * *
Mythic story of good versus evil and the true nature of power. The greatest story outside of the Bible.

Richard Wurmbrand, 1968, *In God's Underground* (Autobiography) *
The life story of a Lutheran pastor who spent 14 years in a communist prison for preaching his faith. Full of wonderful anecdotes.

Non-Academic Non-Fiction
Robert Barron, 2011, *Catholicism* * *
Very readable explanation of the best aspects of Catholicism.

Victor Frankl, 1946, *Man's Search for Meaning* * *
Frankl was a Jewish psychiatrist who survived Auschwitz. His experience led him to write this book on the human need for meaning.

C.S. Lewis, 1952, *Mere Christianity* * *
Probably the clearest defence of Christian Faith. Explaining the core beliefs in simple language.

C.S. Lewis, 1940, *The Problem of Pain* * *
My chapter 14 (Pain, Suffering and God) is basically a summary of this book.

Richard Rohr, 2003, *Everything Belongs*, 2019, *The Universal Christ*, 2016, *The Divine Dance* * *
These three books explore the mystical way of knowing, the *logos* principle and the Trinity.

Academic
Albert Camus, 1942, *The Myth of Sysiphus* * * * *
An essay (not a book). Makes explicit what Camus expresses in "The Plague".

John Carol, 2001, *The Wreck of Western Culture* * * *
Whilst some of his positions are contentious, this book tries to chart the philosophical debates around the rise and fall of the modern paradigm.

Pope Francis, 2015, *Laudato Si.* * *
Encyclical where Pope Francis spells out a Christian vision based on humility, care for the Earth, and a rejection of consumerism and exploitation.

Roger Haight, 1990, *Dynamics of Theology* * * * *
How to do theology. The concepts of symbolic language, metaphors and transcendence all come this book.

Hans Kung, 1993, *Credo* * * *
Probably Kung's simplest work. He steps us through the Apostles creed, unpacking the central beliefs of Christianity.

Hans Kung, 1995, *Christianity* * * * *
An attempt to explain 2000 years of Christian thought. From the apostolic church to the collapse of the Modern paradigm.

Hans Kung, 1974, *On Being a Christian* * * * *
A comprehensive exploration of what it means to be a Christian.

Jose A. Pagoda, *Jesus: An Historical Approximation* * * *
A scholarly investigation into the life, and teaching of Jesus.

William P. Loewe, 1996, *The College Student's Introduction to Christology* * *
Christology is the study of the significance of Jesus. Who he is and why he matters.

Collapse of Civilisation
Jem Bendell, 2018, Deep Adaptation * *
https://jembendell.com/2019/05/15/deep-adaptation-versions/
A conceptual academic paper calling on readers to reassess their work and life in the face of near-term societal collapse.

William Catton Jnr., 1980, *Overshoot* * *
A relatively simple explanation of the delusion at the heart of modernity. Infinite growth on a finite planet is impossible.

John Michael Greer, 2008, *The Long Descent* * *
Explores the nature of civilisational collapse. Civilisations don't fall quickly. They go down in steps over many years.

Nate Hagens, 2025, *The Great Simplification:* * *
https://www.thegreatsimplification.com
Leading academics discuss the polycrisis in Industrial Society.

Pablo Servigne et al, 2015, *How Everything Can Collapse.* * * *
A comprehensive exploration of the polycrisis in industrial civilisation.

For emotional support: Deep Adaptation Forum
https://www.deepadaptation.info

www.ingramcontent.com/pod-product-compliance
Lightning Source LLC
Chambersburg PA
CBHW022043290426
44109CB00014B/962